ALSO BY JOHN ELDER

The Smart Startup: How To Crush It Without Falling Into The Venture Capital Trap

Learn Ruby On Rails For Web Development

PHP Programming For Affiliate Marketers

Intro To Ruby Programming: Beginners Guide Series

Adsense Niche Sites Unleashed

Social Media Marketing Unleashed

SEO Optimization: A How To SEO Guide To Dominating The Search Engines

LIVING THE DOTCOM LIFESTYLE

THE ULTIMATE GUIDE TO INDEPENDENCE
AND FINANCIAL GLORY

JOHN ELDER

Codemy.com
Las Vegas NV

LIVING THE DOTCOM LIFESTYLE

The Ultimate Guide To Independence And Financial Glory

By John Elder

Published By Codemy.com

LAS VEGAS, NV USA

ISBN 0692745777

First Edition

DISCLAMER

All material contained in this book is for informational purposes only and is no substitute for professional advice. Neither John Elder, Codemy.com or it's affiliates (collectively referred to as COMPANY) make any guarantees of the tactics or strategies described in this book. Successful use of any tactic or strategy described in this book depends on the specific person, their experience, and their business and marketing ability. COMPANY makes no claims or guarantees regarding income generated from the use of any tactic or strategy described in this book. Reader agrees to indemnify and hold COMPANY harmless from and against any and all claims, demands, liabilities, expenses, losses, damages, attorney fees arising from any and all claims and lawsuits for libel, slander, copyright, and trademark violation as well as all other claims resulting from reading this book.

For Cindy

CONTENTS

LIVING THE DOTCOM LIFESTYLE

CHAPTER ONE

* * *

INTRODUCTION

"Can you imagine
for a second
doing anything
just 'cuz you want to?
Well, that's just what I do
so hurray for me...
...and FUCK YOU!"

- Hurray For Me
Bad Religion

My name is John, I'm 38 years old and I've never had a job in my entire life.

Not ever.

Nada, zip, zilch. Sure, I've taken the odd freelance consulting gig every now and then when people offered me shit-tons of money for basically no real work for a very short period of time (hey I like free money as much as the next guy), but 99% of the rest of the time I've never had a real job, never had a boss, never had a commute, never had to deal with asshole co-workers or office politics. Nothing, nada, zip, zilch. Let me explain...

When I was 18 years old I dropped out of college after one semester and started one of the Internet's first advertising network websites. The year was 1996, most people had never even heard of the Internet back then and when I told people I was going to build a platform that allowed businesses to easily advertise on the Internet, people *literally* laughed me out of the room. "Why would a business want to advertise on the Internet?!" they all said.

Yeah people are stupid sometimes, but back then online

advertising really was a stretch. Businesses just *weren't* advertising online yet. There was no Google back then, no Youtube, certainly no Facebook; Yahoo barely existed and had just moved off the Stanford web servers onto their own domain name.

It was the wild west.

Come to find out, businesses *did* start to advertise online and my little ad network blew up. I sold it to a publicly traded company at the height of the first dotcom stock market bubble for buckets of money.

Hurray for me.

Then I quickly built a little biotech portal website. It was going to be the "Yahoo of the Biotech world". Basically it aggregated information on the biotech investment community. The site took me about two months to build and another month or so to sell to a group of investment bankers for buckets of money.

Hurray for me again.

After that I developed some desktop Search Engine Marketing software that would automatically submit a website to all the major search engines in seconds. It was called the Submission-Spider. There were like twenty search engines back then (before Google came along and crushed the industry – now there are basically just two search engines; Google and Bing).

The software took me the better part of a long three day weekend to build and ended up being used by over *three million* people, small businesses, and even governments.

Hurray for me again.

After that I got interested in affiliate marketing so I built a network of over 4,000 websites, each focused on a different product niche. Think garden hoses, lawn mowers, kitchen plates, exercise equipment, etc. etc. If you can think of a home and garden product, I probably had a website dedicated to that product.

The sites were very simple, I built some scripts that would auto-generate millions of pages for each website, and each page would target a narrow long tail search keyword, auto-generate some spun text to describe the product, and stick a big button that let you order the thing from Amazon. The sites were also plastered with Google Adsense ads.

Since each site had millions of auto-generated pages about the most esoteric of long-tail keywords, it was pretty easy (at the time) to get ranked fairly well at Google for those keywords.

Why? Because no one else had a page of a website dedicated to the John Deere 27 inch adjustable blade trim attachment with disposable liner in the color yellow! No one. So if someone went to Google and typed in "John Deere 27 inch adjustable blade trim attachment with disposable liner in the color yellow", the chances were pretty freakin' good that my site would show up ranked first in the search results.

Granted, only about two or three people would search for such a phrase each month...but with

4,000 websites and millions of pages for each site, you only needed a handful of visitors per day per site to earn some serious ad revenue from the Adsense ads and Affiliate revenue from the Amazon links.

At the time, Amazon paid me around 7% of the purchase price for everything that people bought after clicking on one of the Amazon links on any of my 4,000 websites.

The sites were all built automatically, the traffic came in automatically, the checks from Amazon and Google Adsense were deposited automatically into my checking account... For the better part of a year I sat on the beach while hundreds of dollars flooded into my checking account every single day.

Hurray for freakin me again.

Eventually Google updated their algorithm to make it much harder to rank crappy spammy sites like that and the income didn't really warrant the expenditure in webhosting and bandwidth so I shut it all down. But it was fun for a while!

Somewhere along the way I decided to go back to college and get a degree; more for fun than anything else. I applied and somehow got into Washington University in St. Louis which at the time was the eighth ranked college in America and knocked out a degree in Economics that took me a little less than three years to complete. Somehow or other I managed to graduate with honors to boot. Washu costs around $60,000 a year, but I had Internet money so I didn't really care about the cost.

After that I started blogging and writing books about different Internet Marketing and computer programming topics (like PHP coding, Ruby on Rails, and stuff like that). People seemed to dig them so I kept writing them.

Then the whole MOOC thing hit (Massive Open Online Courses). Online learning quickly became a huge juggernaut so I started messing around in that area. The "Open" part of MOOC sort of offended my delicate sensibilities, so I decided to charge money for *my* Massive *Closed* Online Courses. MCOC? Coining it!

I built several pretty successful online membership sites that teach different video courses on Internet

Marketing and coding since that's what I have the most experience with.

My latest site is Codemy.com where I've got a bunch of video courses I recorded that teach people how to build websites, and all the different aspects of starting and growing an online business. The coolest part though is the community. People watch the videos, but what they really need is a sounding board for their ideas, and someone to point them in the right direction along the way by answering the zillions of questions that always come up whenever you start any sort of business.

So now I spend a good chunk of my time just answering people's questions at Codemy.com. I've seen and done it all online and I can usually get people sorted out and pointed in the right direction pretty quickly.

It's really fun to help people get their own online businesses up and running. Since these days I can spend my time pretty much however I want; what better way to spend my day than by helping others do what I've done? Besides, you can only hang out on the beach for so long before you lose your mind to boredom.

But enough hoo-ha...you don't care about me *one bit*. The only reason I made you suffer through all that flatulent self-indulgent bragging biography crap is so that you have some idea of my background.

Why?

Because. There are many people

online selling the idea of the dotcom lifestyle.

"GET RICH QUICK!" they all say. But if you look into their backgrounds, nine times out of ten the only real success they've ever had is in selling books or courses that teach people to get rich online. That's not someone you want to learn from because those people usually just rehashing the same old bullshit that doesn't really work.

Me, on the other hand...well I'm someone that's never had a real job. I've made 100% of my income online for almost twenty years...and I've done it by building real businesses that sell real products.

In this book I'm going to teach you the *REAL* way to make money online. Not the guru way, not the flash in the pan way, but the actual honest to goodness tried and true methods that I've used for decades to make tons of money while I hang out at Starbucks sipping overpriced coffee...or at the beach. Chicago (where I lived until recently when I moved to Vegas), ironically, has a couple really nice beaches along Lake Michigan right in the city.

This is going to be a book of *substance*, not fluff. I'm going to lay out step-by-step actionable things that you need to do...scratch that...*must* do, in order to build a successful online business.

Sure I'll sprinkle in some bullshit about sitting on the beach because hey, I spend a lot of time sitting on the beach...that's really what this is all about when you get right down to it. Right?

But before you get to sit on the

beach, you need to build the business...so that's what we'll mainly focus on in this book.

Is it going to be easy? Not necessarily. It'll be easier than you might think...but not as easy as those popular Internet Marketing gurus would have you believe. There won't be any point and click instant profits in this book.

If you're looking for overnight riches with no work involved...look elsewhere. You don't get anything for free in this world and anyone who tells you otherwise is trying to sell you something.

But if you stick with me, follow my instructions, and put in the work...you'll find that it's really hard to actually fail.

I'll teach you the safeguards that you'll need to put in place that minimize the risk of failure, and allow you to learn from any failure that you might encounter, and grow stronger from it.

My business startup methods minimize initial investment. So you won't have to spend much (if any) money to start your online business. That way, if it tanks...you aren't out anything and you can pick up the pieces and try again.

That alone makes it *very* hard to fail in the long run.

Dotcom Lifestyle Axiom #1

If you don't spend much money to start your online business, you can fail often, learn from your mistakes, and try again. You'll win eventually!

I'll teach you my methods and methodologies; and even more importantly - my *philosophy* of starting online businesses. My methods are quite different from both the standard Internet Marketing crowd, as well as the fancy Silicon Valley Venture Capital based startup crowd.

We're going to cover a broad range of topics in this book, so try to stick with me.

I think it'll be worth your time.

So What Exactly *Is* The Dotcom Lifestyle?

Ask ten people that question and you'll likely get ten different answers. To me, living the dotcom lifestyle means freedom and financial independence.

Financial independence gives you the freedom to do whatever you want, whenever you want. It means having complete control over your *time*. If you want to work on your website, you can work on your website. If you want to go hang out on the beach for the day, you can hang out on the beach for the day.

It also means mobility.

I can work from anywhere in the world, all I need is my laptop. If I feel like hopping on a plane and jetting down to South America for a month, all I have to do is throw some clothes in a bag and grab my Macbook; and out the door I go.

My income won't suffer one bit because of that.

THAT'S the important thing! The dotcom lifestyle allows you to build businesses that run more or less on auto-pilot. Sure, you have to keep an eye on things and tweak stuff now and then, but you don't have to punch the 9 to 5 clock in any way - shape - or form.

My father is a dentist. He's owned his own dental practice for 35 years. He considers himself a business owner.

But he's not.

Why? Because the business completely fails the moment he walks out the door. If he's not there to torture people and their teeth, *no income comes in*. If he decides to take a month long vacation, he loses a month's worth of income because he sees no patients during that time.

So he's not really a business owner in the most important sense of the term, he's just an employee.

It's actually worse than being a regular employee because regular employees at most companies get paid vacations and paid sick days... he doesn't!

Dotcom Lifestyle Axiom #2

Being a slave to your business is just as bad as being an employee.

You can make sure that those sorts of things never happen to you if you live the dotcom lifestyle. Freedom, financial independence, and mobility are the cornerstones of the whole thing, don't forget that!

I don't own an alarm clock.

Well, my phone probably has an alarm app on it, but I don't use it to wake up in the morning. Instead, I just wake up whenever my body wakes up.

Want to know something that's really messed up? I usually get up at 5 AM, even on the weekends.

When you've got a job that you hate, the alarm clock is the most miserable thing in the world. You can't *stand* that horrible noise; you dread it, you hate it, you want it to stop forever.

But a funny thing happens when you live the dotcom lifestyle.

Life becomes fun!

I can't wait to wake up every morning because my days are just...fun! I can do whatever I want, whenever I want...and there's a shit ton of stuff I want to do - so I can't wait to get up and get started.

When you live a stress free lifestyle with no one telling you what to do, mornings aren't dreadful anymore.

Sure, I sleep late every now and then; whenever I feel like it. But I rarely feel like it.

I'm not saying you need to wake up at 5 AM. The point is; you can wake up whenever the hell you want...the day is yours to do with what you will. That's the magic of the dotcom lifestyle.

When I first moved to Chicago back around 1999-2000, I was often in the routine of working through the night. My apartment at the time was a block away from Oak Street beach in the Gold Coast of downtown Chicago. So I'd work in my apartment through the night and then I'd head down to the beach at dawn and watch the sun come up. Then I'd make my way back home and go to sleep. I'd wake up around noon or 1:00 in the afternoon and do it all over again. I worked like that for a good solid couple of years and really enjoyed those sun rises over the beach.

The point is, over time my sleep patterns have changed. With the dotcom lifestyle you can live however the hell you want. And that's the whole point.

The World Has Changed

It's not a cliché; the world really has changed in the last decade (or less). You can't count on your job anymore. There's just no such thing as job security at all. These days even the best and the brightest shuffle between two, three, five, even ten jobs throughout their lifetimes.

And more often than not, people are being shuffled right out of their jobs completely.

Non-adjusted government stats tell us that unemployment and underemployment figures are off the charts.

Jobs are being outsourced, consolidated, part-timed, or even completely sent offshore; and none of those trends show any sign of slowing down anytime soon. We don't even need to talk about the trend towards automation and artificial intelligence. In twenty years the robots will be doing everything!

These days it's more important

than ever to be able to supplement or completely replace the portion of your income that comes from a regular job.

Not only that; but the largest generation of people this country has ever seen - the baby boomers - are getting ready to retire soon. Not to be dark, but they're also going start kicking the bucket soon. It's a morbid thought, but it's a reality that will dramatically alter the scope of the economy in this country and even throughout the entire world, and it's coming sooner than most people think.

With a net savings rate close to zero, those retiring baby boomers are in for a nasty surprise come retirement time (that is – the ones that MAKE it to retirement and don't get pushed aside even before that because of ageism).

Why is this so important? If the largest portion of your population is suddenly out of work, but has no savings and is merely squeaking by on their social security payments (as many studies suggest), what happens to all those businesses that used to sell those people all sorts of widgets? If the baby boomers aren't buying (and they won't be), that means jobs building and selling widgets will start to evaporate.

It's a simple matter of supply and demand. Without demand for products bought by baby boomers, supply of labor to make those products will decline dramatically. Things are going to get nasty.

It's just so important to have a source of income that you control and not be stranded at the whim of the slumping labor market or stuck in the ass end of the baby boomer demographic shift that's coming.

What better skill to have than the ability to build an online business that supports you and your family? Better yet, what better skill to have than the ability to build an online business that sells products and services *globally* and isn't tied into the potentially soon to plunge American economy?

This book is all about tools. I'm going to give you the tools to build your own future.

Let's get started...

CHAPTER TWO

***

WHAT DO YOU WANT TO DO?

A couple of months ago my little brother bought a scooter. He's a cardio x-ray tech at a hospital. The moment he bought the thing, he started bugging me about buying one too.

When I was a kid, my best friend Wes put the motor from something or other (I think maybe it was from an electric weed-eater or vacuum cleaner or something like that) on the back of a bicycle. It actually worked, but since it was electric, you needed a bunch of extension cords just to ride the thing around the yard.

That got us thinking; why not use something that doesn't need an electric cord?

Somehow we zeroed in on a gas powered chainsaw, found one at a yard sale for a few bucks, and immediately began hacking away on our own makeshift moped.

It "sort of" worked...but we needed to weld something and neither of us knew how to weld or owned a welder. So we took our contraption down the street to my uncle, who had his own workshop set up in his garage.

My uncle owned a motorcycle, so he immediately fell in love with our little project and immediately co-opted it away from us.

Over the next month or two he tricked out our little chainsaw powered bicycle with a muffler, an actual clutch on the handlebars, and some other things to make the thing work really well.

It.Was.Awesome.

We couldn't have been more than twelve or thirteen years old at the time and suddenly we had our own gas powered bicycle.

Of course, it was only awesome for a few days. Then the police noticed us puttering around town and abruptly shut the whole thing down.

Later on in high school, Wes bought himself an actual motorcycle and drove it around for a few years but I never did. In fact, I hadn't thought about our little moped experiment much at all until my brother bought that scooter and started bugging me to buy one too.

All of a sudden I remembered how much fun we had zipping around on that little chainsaw bike.

I'm not really a scooter kind of guy, but a motorcycle...now that's something I could get behind.

The more I thought about it, the

more I wanted a motorcycle.

Granted I've never actually driven a real motorcycle, in fact I don't know the first thing about them.

So I started to do a little research online, and quickly discovered that you need a motorcycle license to drive a motorcycle. To get the license you have to pass a written test and a driving test at the DMV.

There's also a motorcycle rider program safety course that you can take, and in Illinois (where I was living at the time) it was actually free. If you take the class and pass their written and riding tests, you can get a waiver that lets you automatically get your motorcycle license from the DMV without needing to take the DMV written or riding test (which is harder).

So I went online and found the nearest class, and discovered that there was one starting that very day, in just a couple hours and lasted a week. The class was four hours a day for five days (they also had weekend classes but it was Monday and I didn't want to wait till the weekend).

Unfortunately the class was listed as full.

"Fuck it", I thought to myself "I'm going anyway".

So I dropped what I was doing and jumped in the car. I got to the place and walked in. The two instructors for the class were setting up the classroom. I told them I wanted to take the class but hadn't registered, and asked if there was any way they could squeeze me in.

They told me that if someone

didn't show up, I could take their place – and we'd just have to wait and see.

So I settled in to wait. Sure enough, several people who registered didn't bother to show up so I got in.

To make a long story short, I spent the whole week riding motorcycles for three to four hours a day – which was great because I really had no idea what the hell I was doing. But I'm a quick study and before the week was over I was riding like a pro.

I passed the course tests no problem, and the next day drove over to a local motorcycle shop and bought a used motorcycle. I thought a used bike would be better than a new one because most people say that there's a pretty good chance you're going to dump your first bike at some point – so why wreck a brand new bike when you could wreck a used one instead?! Besides, I had only been riding for a week at that point, and I didn't know what kind of bike I would like best...so something used made sense to me.

So now I own a motorcycle.

In just the first week, I managed to put about 500 miles on the thing. It's been a blast!

Why am I wasting your time with this story? *Because it's important.* If you think about it, the whole thing is ridiculous...

I don't need a motorcycle, but I *wanted* one.

I had no earthly idea how to ride a motorcycle, but I dropped everything and learned.

That week, I spent all day watching youtube videos about motorcycles and reading forum posts from newbie riders. Then I spent four hours in the evening at my rider class. Then I spent the next week riding my bike off and on all day. I didn't do a bit of real work during those two weeks.

Being able to drop everything and do something stupid and fun is the point of my life, it's the point of the dot com lifestyle.

That kind of freedom is hard to explain. I can tell you stories like this till I'm blue in the face, but until you experience it yourself... you just can't know.

It's not even really about being rich. The motorcycle course was free. The used motorcycle only cost a few thousand dollars. I didn't need to be a millionaire to do any of this stuff.

What this is about is *freedom*.

Now that I have my motorcycle, I intend to tour the country a bit. I'll throw some clothes and my laptop in a backpack, hop on my bike, and just drive till I get tired of driving.

I'll be able to stop and work on my laptop in cool places along the way whenever I want. I'm even thinking about getting a little GoPro video recorder to stick on my helmet so I can shoot some videos along the way. How cool would it be to teach Internet marketing from the back of a motorcycle?

So that's what I'm going to do until I get tired of that and switch to something else.

What would you do if you had complete financial freedom? What would you do if you could do anything at all?

Every morning when I wake up, I hear a little voice in my head that asks the same question every single day. The question?

What do you want to do today?

CHAPTER THREE

***

WHAT TO BUILD

I know what you must be thinking at this point:

"This all sounds great, but how do I actually make money online?"

It's a good question, and one that we need to address before we move on.

There are tons of ways to make money online, and new ways are being dreamt up every day. In this chapter I'm going to try to zero in on a few of the most basic methods for building online income and then we'll move on and talk about how to actually build the things we discussed in this chapter later on in the book.

I don't like to think of this as "Making Money Online". Instead, I like to think of it as "Building Businesses Online".

That's essentially what you'll be

doing...building a business. The business will just happen to operate online. It's no different than building any other business.

If you look at it that way, it cuts out a lot of the "get rich quick" type online gimmicks.

So stop asking how to make money online. Instead, start asking yourself what people need.

The core of every single business that was ever built is *need*. Being an entrepreneur is all about identifying a need and filling it. Focus on people...not business.

What do *people* need? What do people want? Is there some need that people have that isn't being met? Can you meet that need? Can you do it online?

I really want you to shift your attention and focus in that way.

Years ago when I first built my search engine submission software, there were over twenty search engines and if you were a website owner and wanted to list your site on those twenty search engines, it was a real pain in the ass to do it manually.

You had to make a list of all those search engines and then hunt around on each of them to find their "submission" page. Then you had to fill out a form (or several forms) and sometimes jump through other hoops too.

It was a pain in the ass.

People were constantly complaining about it on forums. Others were confused by submission guidelines.

Building software that automated the whole process of

submitting a website to all those search engines was a no brainer.

People wanted it. They were vocal. I barely had to market the software, people were already clamoring for it.

Problem and solution.

That's how you should look at any online business you build. Is there a problem? Is there some unmet need? Can you meet some currently met need better and cheaper than what's already out there?

Start by identifying a market – a group of people interested in something.

The market for my search engine software was "website owners". Website owners hang out at webmaster forums, they read webmaster newsletters, they are easy to find, easy to identify, and easy to advertise to.

Even if you only want to dabble in Affiliate Marketing (promoting other people's products or services), you still need to approach it in this same way. Otherwise, how do you determine which products or services to promote?

Identifying a need is one of the most crucial skills to master. We'll discuss some tools that will help you out in this area later on in the book. The Internet is great at giving you data, and there are many free tools you can use to research potential markets.

So keep all of that in mind from now on. Think people first, then business. Look for a need that isn't being met or is being met poorly. Everything else will flow from that.

The Biggest Mistake...

I see this all the time. It is quite possibly the biggest mistake newbies make and it can destroy your chances for success before you even begin.

I'm talking about "following your passion".

You love knitting socks and want to build an online business selling the socks you knit.

You love radio controlled airplane kits so you want to build a website selling them.

Your mother makes amazing cakes so you think maybe she should be selling them on a website.

You like, *you* think, *you* want. It's the entire wrong way to look at things.

Passion is important. But your

opinions and your passions are wholly and completely irrelevant.

This isn't about YOU, it's about your customers.

If you go into this with the mindset of "what you want" and not with the mindset of "what the customers want" then you've already lost.

Like I just said, you have to start by identifying an unmet need. Find something that a group of people are already clamoring for, and then find a way to give it to them. Period.

What are the chances that there are a group of vocal people online desperate for your moms cake, or your knit socks, or the type of radio controlled airplane kits you like? The chances are zero.

But this is what newbies always

do. And then they can't figure out why their business failed.

Identify a need. Nothing else matters.

Types Of Online Businesses

So let's start off by discussing several different types of online businesses that you could build. One or more of them may appeal to you, and the type that appeals to you the most will directly affect how you move forward.

So let's just list a few of the basic types of online businesses.

1. Sell a Product

2. Sell a Service

3. Affiliate Marketing

4. Advertising Based Media

5. Ecommerce

So let's talk about each of these areas a little bit. I'm sure there are other ways to make money online, but I think these five broad ways are more than enough to get you started. They may seem like common sense, but once we dive into them a little deeper, I think you'll be surprised how much area they really cover and how many different options they really give you.

SELL A PRODUCT

You can always sell something. What? Who knows! You can build something yourself, you can buy something from someone else and re-sell it at a profit, you can license something; really the sky is the limit.

Building your own product to sell is the ultimate in online income creation. Why? Because you control everything. Subsequently, it's also probably the hardest. Why? Because you control everything.

The thing you sell can be a physical product; some sort of widget that you manufacture or hire someone else to manufacture. It could also be something electronic like software, or an app, or something like that. It could be a book that you write, or a membership site that you create. Do you have some knowledge that other people would like to learn?

Boom, build a membership site teaching them that knowledge.

There are infinite products that you can sell, and it's not my place to tell you what you should be selling. But I will give you the tools you'll need to sell your product, no matter what that product is.

To sell a product online, no matter what the product, you'll need a website, the ability to accept payment in the form of credit cards, and some way to keep in touch with customers (probably via email).

This is nearly universal no matter what you sell. The obvious exception is if you sell your product through an online marketplace like eBay or even Amazon (in which case you might not really need your own website, and they will likely take care of payment and customer communication themselves).

Many people are hesitant to jump in and start selling their own product, and the costs of getting started might be a little more than some of the other methods that we'll discuss.

But the benefits are the greatest. We'll talk more about building your own product later on in the book.

SELL A SERVICE

Similar to selling a product is selling a service. There are tons of things that you can do online that other people are willing to pay for.

Writing is one thing that pops to mind right away (probably because I'm a writer).

People are always paying for

blog posts, articles, sales letters, you name it. Writing online is a big business and if you're a writer it's relatively easy to find freelance work.

Consulting is also pretty big online. If you have some sort of knowledge that can be applied to a business, those businesses are hungry to hire you.

These could be marketing related things like social media consulting, or SEO consulting, or email marketing consulting.

Or they could be niche industry things. I mentioned that my dad is a dentist. He got a letter in the mail a few weeks ago from some guy who specialized in building and marketing websites for Dentists.

Chances are you've had a job most of your life. So you know

something about it. Can you find some way to consult to others in your field? Think about it.

Earlier I touched upon the problem with selling a service, no matter what that service is. Namely; your income is tied to the clock. If you don't perform the service, you don't get paid.

I prefer to make money while I sleep, 24/7, rain or shine.

If I'm selling a product, I can automate the entire process so that it runs without me. You can't really do that when you're selling a service.

It's not *impossible*, it's just really hard. Technically, you could hire employees to perform the service and in that way you could continue to make money even when you aren't there... but that's a whole other complicated thing.

Selling services is a good way for people who are just starting out online and need cash right away.

People often say to me "I need to make $1,500 right away...how can I do that?" Or sometimes it's $500, or $1,000.

I always answer them by telling them to sell a service. There are places like fiverr.com where you can sell services for $5. Sure, it's not much money, but the jobs are usually very small, so you can stack ten or twenty into a day. $5 times 20 is $100 a day, times six days a week is $600, times four weeks a month is $2,400.

Sure you're not going to get rich and it's going to be tedious and boring work, but if you need to make rent in a hurry it can work.

There are many sites like fiverr.com out there that allow you to sell your services. Just search around with Google to find a site that specializes in whatever service you're trying to sell.

Again, this isn't something I really recommend if you're trying to live the dot com lifestyle, but it can be a good way to ease into things and supplement your income while you figure things out.

AFFILIATE MARKETING

Affiliate marketing is the promotion of other people's products or services. Generally, affiliate marketers receive a percentage of the sale price of whatever they sell. Depending on the program, that percentage can vary from as low as 4-5% to upwards of 50-75% depending on the product and/or company.

A lot of people who are just starting out online tend to gravitate towards affiliate marketing because it has a very low barrier to entry.

You don't necessarily need to build a website, you don't need to set up order processing (ie you don't need to accept credit cards), you don't need to worry about order fulfillment, and you don't have to deal with any sort of customer support. The company who owns the product takes care of all that.

Usually you'll get your own affiliate URL which is a unique URL assigned only to you. Any orders that come from that URL get credited to you.

Think: www.domain.com/JS824

Or something like that...the JS824 thing at the end is your Unique ID. Now you can promote that URL and when someone clicks on it and buys whatever you're selling, you get a percentage of the sale price.

There are all sorts of affiliate marketing programs out there. Places like ClickBank allow you to select and promote specific products, or you can go broader and sign up as an Amazon.com affiliate and sell any or all of the products offered on Amazon.

As a rule of thumb, usually when an affiliate program is very specific (like selling just one product ie Clickbank) you can expect higher commissions. When the program is very broad (like Amazon's affiliate program) you can expect much lower commissions.

Amazon, for instance, uses a sliding scale based on how many items you sell in a month. Sell just a few items and they'll only pay you like 2-4%, sell more and the payout increases to 5-7% or more.

Still, 7% is not much. If you sell $10,000 worth of products through Amazon, you might only receive $700 in affiliate commissions.

But affiliate marketing can be very lucrative if you play it right. The problem is; most people don't play it right.

I recommend treating affiliate marketing like an actual business. Build your own website, create your own email lists, build your own brand, and at the last moment filter your customer to your affiliate URL. We'll talk more about this exact thing later on in the book.

ADVERTISING BASED MEDIA

Another popular business model is the Advertising based model. Basically, you earn your money by selling advertising.

There are several different ways to play this one. You could build a blog about some specific niche. You could build a Youtube channel about some specific niche. You could combine the two and build a video blog (vlog) that you host.

The trick is to build a *platform* (blog, youtube channel, twitter following, whatever), and build an *audience*.

Then you monetize that traffic with advertising. Most people start out with generic Google Adsense ads, and eventually move up to selling ad space directly to advertisers. The more niche your blog is, the easier it is to sell advertising.

For example, if you have a blog that's all about applying makeup, and 50,000 happy teens tune in every time you post a blog update, then it's going to be pretty easy to sell ad space to makeup companies.

Specific Niche + Steady Traffic = Ad Revenue.

This can be a very lucrative business, but it's very hard to crack into. Blogs can take months or years to gain traction, if ever. They don't happen overnight. Can you post blog updates or make a new video every single day for 15 months without getting much traffic at all during all that time and still keep the faith that eventually your blog will catch on? Will you get depressed after six months of daily blog posts with only 47 people reading them each day?

If so, this isn't for you.

Content creation is hard; it's especially hard to do day in and day out, on schedule, and keep things fresh and interesting (that's why Hollywood people make so much money). That's why so many blogs pay people for content (and why you can easily sell your services as a writer if you are so inclined).

On the other hand, if you know how to build an audience, then the advertising model can be like printing money.

ECOMMERCE

Finally, I'll mention ecommerce, which is an overused term that gets thrown about all the time, sometimes incorrectly.

I'm going to define ecommerce as Amazon.com. You know Amazon, they sell just about everything. But the model they use, the site layout, etc... that's ecommerce.

Think of it as creating your own online store that sells lots of different things.

Ecommerce can be a strange combination of several of the business methods I just discussed. You can create an ecommerce store selling your own products, you can build one selling other people's products, and any number of combinations of the two.

The trick with ecommerce, like many other things online, is to pick a niche. Do you understand bow hunting? Build an ecommerce site that sells bows. Do you know Bicycle racing? Build an ecommerce site that sells Bike jerseys. Think Niche. Yes, this contradicts what I said earlier about not building things YOU want, instead building things others want...but ecommerce is an exception because you're going to blanket the site with tons of products.

Something popular that I'm seeing more and more these days (but I haven't tried yet myself) is to source inventory from China via Alibaba.com (which is sort of like the Amazon.com of China but for bulk items).

Alibaba.com allows you to order whole crates of things very cheaply. So people buy a pallet of toe-nail clippers for .07 cents each and then build a toe-nail clipper ecommerce store selling them for $5 each and then pocket the difference. You get the idea.

If you can find a niche and a market and a good supplier on Alibaba, you can make good money doing this, but there are some downsides as well.

You need cash to start this sort of business...cash to order your inventory from China. Generally you can't order 5 of something' you have to order 500 of something, or 1,000 of something etc. So if the thing doesn't sell, you're out of luck.

Also, you have to store your inventory. You might start out storing your inventory in your spare bedroom or garage, but at some point if you're successful, you're going to need a warehouse of some sort.

This can quickly turn into a full-fledged business.

On the other hand, you can choose to merge affiliate marketing with ecommerce and build your own ecommerce store stacked full of products from, say, Amazon.com. Your website looks like your own store, but when someone finally decides to buy and clicks on the order button, they get transported to Amazon.com and you earn your little 4-7% commission.

Either way, ecommerce tends to

be something that takes a little more knowledge and experience to pull off so I generally try to steer newbies away from it until they have a little more experience.

So there you have it, five basic methods for making money online. Sure they might have been overly broad, but we'll dive deeper into each of them throughout this book. I think you'll come to realize that they're a pretty good jumping off point for those of you just getting started, and a pretty good place to start even for those of you with a little more experience online.

In the next chapter I'll spend a little bit of time on mindset and philosophy, and then we'll dive into each of these items and flesh them out in much more detail.

CHAPTER FOUR

✳✳✳

SOME PHILOSOPHY

Before we dive in and start talking about the specifics of each of those business models I touched on in the last chapter, I want to spend just a couple of minutes talking about basic philosophy.

This is pretty important and I hope you don't blow this part off because it can have a real impact on everything.

I talk to quite a few people every day who want to live the dot com lifestyle. I see a lot of the same things over and over.

People want to dive right in, quit their day job, invest thousands of dollars and hit the ground running.

I think that's a big mistake.

It's much more reasonable to ease your way into this. If you follow my general philosophy, you don't have to invest thousands of dollars, and you don't have to quit your job...at least not right away.

I often get emails from people that look like this:

"I've got $10,000 saved up, how should I spend it? Should I buy an ecommerce site? Should I spend it on advertising? Help!"

People who invest a ton of money looking for a shortcut almost always fail.

Instead, you should ease into things. Start small! There's no reason to spend thousands of dollars on some readymade scheme that's "guaranteed" to work. They never do.

And there's no reason to spend thousands of dollars to have someone build you a website. I'll show you how to build a very professional looking website for little to no money.

If you ease into things, if you spend your <u>time</u> instead of your money, then you are free to fail. If your business doesn't work, you aren't out anything! You can pick up the pieces and try again.

Every time you fail, I promise that you'll learn something from it. Eventually you'll figure this whole thing out and start making money.

Dotcom Lifestyle Axiom #3

Invest Time…Not Money!

The most important thing to do

is invest your time, not your money. You're already doing that by reading this book. Don't stop!

There are so many free resources online that will teach you anything and everything you could ever want to know about everything you'll need to build cool stuff online.

There are free courses that teach basic web programming, web design, wordpress, etc etc.

The more you can learn on your own, the less you'll have to pay someone else to do the work for you.

It takes time, but it's really worth it in the end.

If I wanted to open a dog grooming business, the first thing I'd do is learn how to groom dogs. I don't know anything about dog grooming. Why would I think I could open a dog grooming business without learning how to groom a dog?

But that's what people do every single day online. They start an online business without learning the basics of web development; how to build a website, how to start an email list, how web hosting works, etc. Why would you think you could start an online business without learning those things?

Sure, you could hire people to do those things for you...but how do you figure out who to hire and how much to pay them? If you don't know what's involved in building a website, and some kid tells you that it's gonna cost $5,000; what do you know!? You don't know that it might only takes that kid a day and a half to build your website and $150 might be a more appropriate fee to pay him.

So learn this stuff. Even if you aren't technologically inclined, spend some time learning as much as you can manage. It'll pay dividends for years to come.

You don't need to learn to be an engineer. But learning the basics of HTML, how web hosting works, how email works, how to process credit cards, and other basics like that will make all the difference. Trust me.

Dotcom Lifestyle Axiom #4

Don't quit your day job!

People romanticize the dot com lifestyle and often want to run out and quit their job and dive right in. That's almost always a mistake. Ease into things!

Spend your nights and weekends building your first online business. I know you're tired after working all day, but this stuff is fun and once you get started the time will fly.

Slowly build up your first online income stream. Don't quit your day job until you can replace your current income with your online income.

Remember, you'll lose your job benefits if you quit your job. You'll have to replace things like health insurance. So even if you manage to build an online income stream that matches your current salary, you'll likely need to earn even more than that online in order to cover the costs of health insurance and business taxes.

Sure it can be done, that's the whole point of this book. I'm just suggesting that you ease into it. Take it one step at a time.

If you keep your day job, don't invest much money in your online startup, and make a commitment to learn as much as you can and keep plugging away...eventually you'll be successful.

It's the slow and steady success that you really want to find. Slow and steady is the only real success. Everything else is just myth and dot com hype.

Sure, I'm a bit of a hypocrite here. I did the exact opposite when I first started. I dropped out of college, sold my car, and rolled the dice.

But I was only eighteen years old at the time and you can take those kind of chances when you're young and don't have any responsibilities. I wasn't married, didn't have any kids, and was young. I wasn't really risking much by jumping in with both feet.

It's completely different if you're married with kids and have a solid career that you might be throwing away.

So ease into things. Learn. Grow stronger. When you start making money, wait still. Don't quit your job until your online income surpasses your current salary (including benefits).

Then, when the time is right and you feel comfortable with the success of your online business, pull the cord and parachute out of that crappy job of yours!

I call this philosophy the "Smart Startup" method and I wrote a book about it called "The Smart Startup: How To Crush It Without Falling Into The Venture Capital Trap". You can check it out at:

www.Codemy.com/ss

That will redirect to the Kindle and paperback version of the book over at Amazon.

The other option is to raise money from a Venture Capitalist. VC's are investors who invest in early stage startups.

The tech VC industry is very popular these days. HBO even made a popular series about it.

Some suggest that it's easier to raise money for a new business today than ever before. That may be true, but I hope you'll resist the urge to go down that path.

When you accept investors into your company, you give up freedom. Don't kid yourself. If someone invests a bucket of money into your company, then they're the ones who will ultimately call the shots and they're the ones who you will answer to...forever.

The point of this whole dot com lifestyle is *freedom*. Having to answer to someone else and do what they say because they own a large chunk of your company doesn't really sound like freedom to me.

Instead, I suggest that you learn to build your own website. It's much much easier than you think, even if you have no tech knowledge at all. There are so many tools that will help you these days (think Wordpress), that it can really be a point and click process.

Sure, the more you learn, the cooler things you can build. But basic websites are pretty easy to build.

I highly suggest you check out my Codemy.com website. I've got lots of video courses where I literally walk you step by step through building websites (both point and click Wordpress sites all the way up to super technical badass Ruby on Rails sites – one course teaches you how to build a clone of Pinterest using Ruby on Rails).

You can take an individual

course for $47 each, or sign up to become a full member and get access to all of them for $147.

As a thank you for reading this book, I'll even knock off $50 bucks from the full membership, you'll pay just $97 to get access to everything.

Just use coupon code **elder41** when you checkout.

Codemy.com is great because it gives you all the knowledge you need to build any kind of website you like, but even better – it gives you direct access to me so that you can ask questions along the way if you get stuck. All free with membership.

It's like having a technical co-founder that you don't have to pay!

Obviously, I recommend you join my website…but if you don't

want to shell out the money to join, I highly recommend that you find SOME place to learn how to build websites.

A basic knowledge will go a long way here and save you a ton of money in the long run.

Like I said earlier, if you can build your own website for free, then you can fail as often as you want. You aren't out any money!

On the other hand, if you have to pay someone to build you a website, and it fails; well... you're just up the creek without a paddle.

I don't want to turn this into a sales pitch (any more than I already have) so I'm going to definitely talk about the basics of building your own website a little later in the book. But if you want an in depth immersion into the subject with hands on help and step by step videos – check out my Codemy.com site.

How Do You Make Money Online?

Later on, I'm going to dive into each of those five business models that we talked about in the last chapter. But right now I want to talk to you about the broad philosophy of making money online.

This will apply to any of the five business models we discussed, or really any business model; online or off.

What makes a business successful?

We've touched on this already when we talked about defining a niche target market; finding a group of people who have some unmet need – and then filling that need.

That's a good place to start.

Whenever you start any sort of business, the first thing is to identify the market.

What type of person is interested in your product? Who are they? Where are they? What are their behaviors? Where do they hang out online? What are their ages? Are they male or female or both?

I recently started to get into freelance television show script writing. The first thing you need to do when writing a script for a television show is to identify your audience. Is the show aimed at kids? Teenagers? Bored housewives? Middle class families? Upper class families? Men? Women?

If you can't figure out who the audience is, watch the commercials that air during the show. Are there commercials for BMW cars and expensive watches? Then the show's audience is upper class men. Are there lots of beer commercials? Then the show's audience is horny young men. Toys? The audience is children. You get the idea...

The audience is *everything*. If you don't know who your audience is, then you can't possibly write a good script...or in our case, build a good business.

Knowing your audience, your niche, your customer is the most important thing for you to focus on from day one.

The second thing to focus on – and this is nearly as important – is your customer's lifetime value.

Here's a secret. No business that only sells one thing to each customer succeeds. The trick is to sell multiple things to each customer over time, forever.

If someone buys something from you and then goes away, it's really hard to build a business around that. Why? Because in order to make more money you have to find more customers...and finding a customer and getting them to buy that first thing is just balls out hard™. It's one of the hardest things in the world to do!

On the other hand, once someone buys something from you once, it becomes INFINITELY easier to sell them something else in the future. In fact, many companies will sell that first product at a loss (called a "loss leader") because they know they'll make up for it by selling more expensive things to that customer in the future.

Think about that…it makes sense! The first time someone buys something from you - especially online – they don't know who you are, they don't know if your product will do what it's supposed to do, hell they don't even know if you're real or some scammer that's going to take their money and sell their credit card number to the Russian Mafia!

But the second time…oh the second time! The second time they DO know all that stuff. You've built trust. You've lived up to and (hopefully) exceeded their expectations.

So let me ask you this... Which is better; to sell one $19.95 widget to one person and then hope to sell another widget to another person and on and on...or to sell a $19.95 widget to one person, and then a few months later sell another $19.95 widget to that same person, and then a few months later to sell a slightly more expensive $39 widget to that same person, and then a year later to sell a $129 widget to that person and then and then and then, forever?

Lifetime value. It's the name of the game. It changes everything if you look at every single customer that way.

If you play your cards right, you might sell $400 worth of stuff to each of your customers on average over the next ten years.

Let me ask you this…if you're going to make $400 per customer (let's just pretend), then how much money can you spend to *acquire* each customer?

The answer is anything less than $400.

Now, obviously you won't know how much you're going to sell to each customer over their useful lifetime, at least not right away…but thinking about it in those terms puts you head and shoulders above most businesses who focus only on short term profits.

Now, to build a business that focuses on lifetime value requires more planning. You need mechanisms that will allow you to follow up with your customers, to build on-going relationships, to get them back to your website over time so that they can continue to buy stuff from you.

Luckily the Internet gives us the tools we need to do that, making it easier than ever before in the history of commerce to build loyal repeat business.

Social media helps out here too (Twitter, Facebook, Instagram, Youtube). These tools allow you to keep in contact with past customers in ways never before dreamed of.

But the real workhorse tool, and it's one that doesn't get much respect these days in the world of shiny glittery social media, is <u>email</u>.

Email marketing is still by and far the best way to build relationships with your customers. Email grows your business, email IS your business. It is the cornerstone of every successful online business that I've ever been involved in. It's not sexy, and it can be frustrating at times (think spam filters). But if you get it right, email can become a gigantic hose that sprays money whenever you turn it on.

Why is email so much better than Social Media? Because you own your email lists. You choose when to send out email and to who. Not so with Social Media. If you post something on your Facebook page, only a small percentage of your followers will see that because Facebook caps that level (unless you pay them extra).

Other social media sites can get bogged down and overwhelming. If you post something on Twitter, how many of your followers will see it? Can you even find out? Sure Twitter (and others) have analytics, but they've never worked all that well.

Email is different.

When you send out email to your list of past customers, you know exactly who gets it. You know exactly who opened it. You know exactly who clicked the link in the email and ordered whatever widget you're promoting.

It's all trackable, to an astonishing degree. Learn to do email marketing correctly and you can generate money at will...it's as easy as sending out an email.

There are many companies that will handle all the nuts and bolts of email marketing for you. Companies like aweber.com or mailchimp.com offer the tools you'll need at shockingly cheap prices. They'll manage your lists, give you stats, automate subscribing and unsubscribing, etc.

Back when I was running my software company selling my Submission-Spider SEO software I had a bunch of email promotions that I'd send out at specific times each year. I tweaked them and worked on them so much over the years that I KNEW how much money each would make before I even sent them out.

One of my favorites was the day after Christmas email. I'd send it out the day after Christmas to all the people who had downloaded the free trial of my software in the last few months, but hadn't actually gone on to buy the software. It went something like this…

"Hi [Name],

A while back you downloaded our Submission-Spider software. For whatever reason, you didn't go on to buy it.

I've gotten myself into a bit of a problem and I wondered if you could help.

This Christmas I went a little overboard on the gifts. I chunked quite a bit on the ole credit card.

It's no big deal really, and I'll be fine either way. But now that Christmas is over I don't really want to face the new year with such a sizeable chunk of debt on my credit card.

I'd like to start the new year off debt free. So I sat down and started brainstorming ways to raise a quick couple of thousand bucks.

And this is what I've come up with.

I hope you decided not to purchase

the Submission-Spider because of the high price tag. That's generally the reason people give us when they decide not to buy the software.

If that's the case, I'd like to offer you a huge discount on the software. This deal is only good for the next couple of days, by which time I hope to have paid off my Christmas credit card debt.

The Submission-Spider is regularly priced $99 on our site. For the next couple of days I'll offer it to you for only $9.99

Yeah I know, that's a crazy discount. But I only need to sell 2 or 3 hundred copies at that price to solve my little problem so I figured - what the heck.

There are no strings attached. You receive the complete registered software for only $9.99 if you order right now *from: URL*

But remember what I said. I only need to sell 2 or 3 hundred copies at the discount price to settle my credit card bill.

After I hit my goal, I'm taking down that special order page and you won't be able to buy the software at the special discount price anymore. So act right now.

I don't know how quickly I'll reach my goal. It may be an hour from now, it may be a day or two.

Order now or you may not make it in time.

I hope you'll take advantage of this great offer because I doubt I'll be offering the software so cheaply any time soon.

I'll also give you a great free gift if you order right away. I'll throw in a copy of my highly popular eBook..."

You get the idea. I sent out that email the day after Christmas for the better part of ten years, and every year it generated THOUSANDS of dollars in extra sales that I wouldn't have earned otherwise.

And that was just one of many emails I had scattered throughout the year. Some gave discounts, some gave information, some were good old fashioned hard sells. The point is, over time I came to understand how much money each of those emails would generate. It became a reliable process. That's what makes it *a business*.

Email is the single most valuable part of any business you create, no matter which of those business models you choose from.

Email allows you to follow up

with past customers and turn them into repeat customers…and repeat customers are the name of the game.

Sure, social media is great, and you'll utilize it. But social media will never become the cornerstone of your business like email marketing will.

Like I said, you don't own your own Facebook page; Facebook does. THEY choose how your message goes out, not you. And they can change the rules at any moment (and they have), at the drop of a hat, to benefit themselves at your own expense.

The dot-com lifestyle is all about freedom and control. Email marketing gives you that, social media does not.

The Marketing Funnel

All of these tactics are part of something that we call the "Marketing Funnel". It's a basic concept in marketing that most first year marketing majors learn.

Think of an ordinary funnel, like you might find in a kitchen, or a mechanics garage.

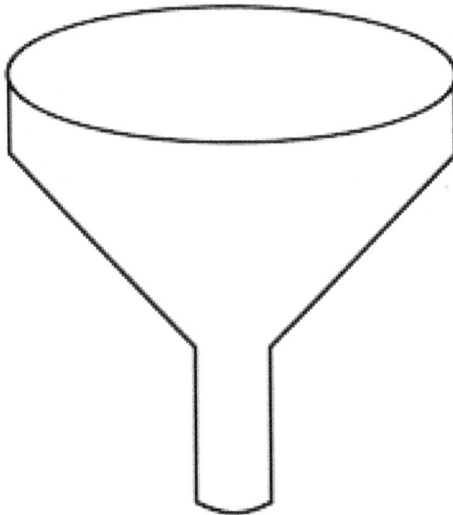

The Marketing Funnel

The top of the funnel is the widest, that's where all your new customers come in. At the top of your funnel, you offer them the cheapest thing that you have to sell (or even something free).

Why cheap? Because of the law of supply and demand, which I'll paraphrase as: "The cheaper a thing is, the more people will buy it. The more expensive a thing is, the less people will buy it." Or as my Intro to Macro Economics professor would say, "The lower the price, the higher the quantity demanded; the higher the price, the lower the quantity demanded".

By offering the cheapest thing to new customers, you hope to lure as many of them into your funnel as possible.

Then they begin their journey

down the funnel.

As they move down, you'll offer them more expensive products. The funnel narrows as it goes down. Why? Because as you offer people more expensive things, less of them will buy. But no worries, that's to be expected.

As time goes on, each customer will move down the funnel, and you'll offer them more and more expensive things. Over time less and less of them will buy the more expensive thing, but that's ok. If 100 people buy something from you for $10, you've made $1,000. If only 8 of those people go on to buy something from you for $249, well that's $1,992 which is quite a bit better than 100 people earning you $1,000.

But you get the idea.

Of course, you'll use email marketing to sell these additional things to the customers in your funnel.

And you may have more than one funnel. You can have infinite funnels. Once your customers get through the sales process of the first funnel, you can dump them into the next funnel, which starts over by offering them some other cheap product.

It's the *concept* that I want you to start to wrap your head around; the concept of offering cheap products to lure the most customers, then selling them increasingly expensive items over time, using email marketing.

That's the heart of the dotcom lifestyle. No matter what you sell; a product, service, affiliate product, ecommerce product of some sort, even advertising... this model applies.

It's the only model that I've found to consistently work. It's the only model I've found the real pros to use.

And what could be easier than a freakin' funnel? Ok, enough philosophy, let's get into specifics.

CHAPTER FIVE

***

SELLING YOUR OWN PRODUCT

Now it's time to dive in and start talking about those five basic business models that I mentioned a couple of chapters ago.

The first model that I want to talk about is "selling a product". Now, this could be something you create, or it could be something that someone else created that you bought or licensed from them.

I'm only going to talk about selling your own product, mainly because selling something that someone else created falls more into affiliate marketing, and I'm going to talk about that later on.

So let's talk about creating your own product...

This is by far the hardest of the five models that we're going to talk about, and that's why I want to tackle it first.

It also has the potential to be the most lucrative of all the models. Why? Because you control everything; and therefore reap all the profits. It also lends itself to scale and automation better than some of the other models (it's hard to scale selling a service).

What Should You Sell?

I have no earthly idea! I couldn't possibly tell you what to sell; you'll have to figure that out yourself. I've given you some hints that it should be something that a group of people are already clamoring for. That's a good place to start.

Here's another piece of advice that I learned early on...

If you want to make millions of

dollars, you have to affect the lives of millions of people.

You aren't going to get rich selling something to a group of a hundred people. You need to target as large a group as possible, but at the same time target minutely.

That is to say, don't target "women". That's too broad (even though there are obviously millions of them). Instead target...new mothers, or recent graduates, or women CEO's. Or whatever! You get the idea...target a specific group, just make sure the group is as large as possible.

Types Of Things To Sell

You could sell some physical product that you need to manufacture...that's pretty hard, especially for someone just starting out who doesn't know what the hell they're doing. Manufacturing is very expensive. And then you have to warehouse those things, and ship them, and insure them, and and and...it's a pain in the ass and not something suited to someone who wants to spend their time lounging on a beach somewhere.

You could sell an app of some sort. Do you know how to program computers? Maybe creating an iphone app of some sort might be up your alley. There's no inventory to worry about there!

You could sell some other sort of digital product like an eBook or online course of some sort. Membership sites are really hot right now. Apart from my Codemy.com website that teaches people to code, I'm also building one together with a buddy of mine that teaches people to play the drums. He's a drummer and music teacher by profession, so we video recorded him giving some beginner drum lessons and slapped them up on a membership website.

These days building a digital product of some sort is the easiest way to go, in my opinion.

Do you have some special knowledge that people might be interested in? Do you have some special skill that you learned at your job that might be transformed into some sort of digital product like a book or membership site?

Digital products are great because there's no inventory, they cost little to create, and they scale easily.

What Do You Need To Get Started?

No matter what sort of product you decide to sell, there are a few things that you're absolutely going to need in order to get started.

First, you're going to need a website of some sort. Luckily a basic business website selling a basic product of some sort is relatively easy to build. I suggest you go with Wordpress, which is a point and click content management system (CMS) that makes building webpages super easy.

Wordpress works with something called "themes". You find a Theme that looks cool to you, upload it to your Wordpress site with the click of a button, and fill out some details to customize it with your specific information, and then walla! You have a professional looking website.

I've got a great video course on building Wordpress sites where I walk you through setting them up and adding themes over at Codemy.com if you want to learn more.

Themes generally cost between $40 and $100 and there are literally thousands to choose from at websites like ThemeForest.net and others.

You don't need any type of programming knowledge to use Wordpress, though if you want to modify your Wordpress site outside the normal bounds of customization - a knowledge of the PHP programming language is useful.

What else will you need? Well, you'll need some way to accept payments. There are basically two choices for you; paypal, or a merchant account.

Paypal is the all-in-one payment processing system that everyone in the world is familiar with. Paypal takes care of everything for you, and charges you a small percentage of each transaction. Customers can choose to pay with their own Paypal account, or with a credit card.

Many Wordpress themes have plugins that integrate Paypal seamlessly, allowing you to set it up with just a few points and clicks.

The other major option is for you to set up a merchant account. A merchant account is something offered by major banks. Generally, you need to have formed your own company (a corporation or LLC) to open a merchant account. We'll talk about the benefits of forming corporations and LLC's later on in the book – hint: you should do it.

Once you have a Merchant account, you'll need to integrate it into your website. There are many third party tools that let you do this, but they're almost all expensive.

Stripe is a good alternative. It's sort of a Merchant Account and web API all wrapped into one…but you need programming experience to set it up. It's definitely NOT point and click. But if you have a little programming experience or can read a tutorial or two and figure it out, Stripe is actually a great option. I use them myself for my sites (I actually use both Stripe AND

Paypal because I find that giving people as many options to pay as possible increases sales).

1shoppingcart.com is a site that integrates merchant accounts with online payment systems, and they've been around forever, but I tend to remember them being a little pricey.

As a newbie just starting out, I suggest you go with Paypal to get started. As you get more customers you can look into other merchant account options.

Why not stick with Paypal? They can be a little expensive, and not all that reliable at times. Some people have had problems with Paypal stealing their money (if you can believe that). If Paypal decides that your product has a high risk of chargebacks or returns (a chargeback is when a customer is not happy and demands their money back straight from Paypal), they can put a hold on your account and freeze all the money in there for months. It's basically stealing, though you'll get the money back eventually; probably. There's not much you can do about it. Google it, there are some real horror stories about this floating around; though it's never happened to me.

Also, I don't remember off hand how much Paypal charges per transaction, but let's pretend it's 3%...well you might be able to find a Merchant account somewhere that only charges 2%. That extra 1% might not matter to you when you're first getting started, but as you get good at this and start making millions of dollars, those percentages add up! 1% of $1 million dollars is $10,000 bucks.

And also, some people just don't like Paypal and don't want to buy something online using it.

So what else will you need?

Well, you'll need some way to stay in contact with your customers, and let them get into contact with you.

There are basically two areas to focus on here; customer support, and marketing.

We've already touched on email marketing a bit already. I recommend mailchimp.com to handle all your email marketing needs.

But what about customer support? As sure as God made little apples, you're going to have pissed off customers who need to get in touch with you.

You could have the best product in the world, and you're still gonna have a slew of pissed off customers. They'll need some way to get in touch with you.

Back in the old days, you needed a phone number and live customer support. As a small business owner, that usually meant 'you' sitting next to the phone dealing with angry customers all day.

It sucked. No one wants to spend their time like that, and it definitely throws a wrench into the whole dot com lifestyle aura.

These days it's different. Customers have been taught to use online email ticketing systems. You open a support ticket, type out your problem, and someone will email you an answer within a day or so.

That's wonderful! It's still not a terrible idea to have a phone number posted on your web site (just to make potential customers comfortable), but funnel all your support through email.

There are tons of email ticketing systems you can set up, many for free that will handle all this stuff.

Then you can either answer the emails yourself, or farm it out to a virtual assistant or an employee.

This isn't going to be a huge problem when you're first starting out because you won't have a lot of customers in the beginning. If 1% of them need to get in contact with you, and you only have 100 customers, well that's not something you're going to have to hire someone to deal with.

But as time goes on and you get more and more customers, you're going to spend more and more time dealing with complaints, and questions, and refunds.

Other than that, there really isn't much that you're going to need. That's the beauty of selling a digital product versus an actual product.

You just need a website, some way to accept money from your customers, and some way for them to get in touch with you (and for you to get in touch with them in the future to sell them more stuff).

And like I said…Wordpress is a great option. There are many Wordpress themes that integrate with both Paypal and merchant accounts (or other online order processing companies). I think there may even be a Stripe Wordpress plugin now.

And Wordpress even makes setting up an online store easy (if you plan on selling more than one item).

I could write an entire book about Wordpress, but you can do a little research on your own. There are tons of free tutorials out there explaining it in great detail, and you can always buy my Wordpress video course over at Codemy.com

No matter what you end up selling, just remember...it's all about the customer, not about what you want to sell. Affect millions to make millions and target closely.

CHAPTER SIX

*****

SELLING YOUR
OWN SERVIVE

Selling a service is much like selling a product in that you're going to need many of the same things. You'll need a website, a way to accept money from your customers, and a way for them to get into contact with you if they need to.

But selling a service is very different than selling a product because you can't really scale that like you can scale a product-based business (well you can, but it's tricky).

I do, however, sometimes recommend this route for someone just starting out if they don't have a lot of money to invest in building their own product, or if they need money right away.

I can't tell you how many times people have come to me and said "I need a quick $1,000 right now, what should I do?!"

I always suggest they sell some service.

There are tons of websites that allow you to sell specific services.

If you know how to build websites or write computer code, or do graphic design work; then websites like freelancer.com are great.

If you have other skills like social media marketing, or graphic design skills, then sites like fiverr.com might be good for you.

If you can write, then sites like upwork.com or even fiverr.com might be worth looking into.

By and large, you aren't going to make a ton of money with these small gigs…heck fiverr.com pays $5 per gig. But they aren't particularly hard either. If you can stack a half dozen or a dozen together per day...you can squeak by with some cash.

Obviously these aren't dot com lifestyle situations (except for the fact that they're done online), but if you're in a pinch and need to make some quick cash...they can work.

If you have more of a business in mind, then you'll want to treat it more like a business. Don't use any of those sites that I mentioned, instead build your own site offering your own services, and go out and find clients yourself.

That's easier said than done and I've never really been a fan.

Besides, like I mentioned earlier; if you aren't there to do the work – you don't make any money. That hardly seems like an ideal situation for someone who wants to spend their days lounging on a beach somewhere.

Is It Possible To Scale A Service Business?

Yes it is! There are a couple of different ways to scale a service-based business.

The first is to simply build an actual company with actual employees. If you've got an office somewhere with twenty people working for you to do all the actual work, as well as people to handle accounting, and manage the employees etc etc, then you can spend your time on the beach.

Of course, you'll have to check in on the asylum every now and then, but generally speaking you can eek out some freedom that way.

That seems like a hell of a lot of work and hassle to me. But it is possible.

The second way to turn a service into a passive income generating business is to somehow turn the service into a SAAS product.

SAAS stands for Software as a Service.

That is, you figure out how to turn the service into a piece of software or web app of some sort…then you sell the web app like any other product.

Obviously you won't be able to turn all services into a software product.

But automation and artificial intelligence (AI) allows us to build software to do a lot of things that once needed people.

So it's getting easier and easier to pull this sort of thing off. There are lots of opportunities to do this if you really put your mind to it.

Plus disrupting old industries is always kind of fun.

One example that I've been thinking about for a while is legal document review.

My ex-wife is a lawyer, and she works in doc review. Basically when company A sues company B, there are millions of documents that need to be read and categorized. For instance, you might look through all the email of company A looking for any mention of XYZ. Major companies generate millions of emails...and the lawyers have to read through all of them.

So basically you have dozens, sometimes even hundreds of lawyers stuck in a little room huddled around computer screens reading email for twelve hours a day, every day. If they see any mention of XYZ in an email, they click a button to flag it and that email gets sent to the next department for review.

Can you imagine how expensive it is to pay hundreds of lawyers to read email and other documents all day looking for specific keywords?

Why isn't there software that will do this automatically?

An enterprising entrepreneur surely will build it someday soon and all of those lawyers will be out of work.

That's a pretty good example of turning a service into software, and

I think you can see how easy it would be to make a small fortune doing something like that. Disruption always brings financial reward to the disruptors.

So if you absolutely must sell a service, I hope you'll do it with an eye towards turning that service into a product of some sort.

Otherwise you're just building a job for yourself...and honestly, you might as well keep your current job because it's probably a lot less stressful than building your own company and dealing with clients yourself day in and day out (not to mention doing the actual service work).

CHAPTER SEVEN

***

AFFILIATE MARKETING

The next business model I want to talk about is Affiliate Marketing. I really like Affiliate Marketing because it lets you dip your feet into this whole nutty world of online commerce without having to spend any money developing your own product.

Basically, affiliate marketing is the act of selling someone else's product and getting a commission.

The amount of the commission depends entirely on what the company is willing to pay you.

Usually the smaller the company and the more niche the product, the higher the commission. Why is that? Smaller companies are willing to pay out more because they're more desperate to sell their products.

Amazon.com doesn't need your

help selling their products, so you can bet their affiliate program pays a low percentage (2% to 8%).

On the other hand, if Bob over there builds some cool software and doesn't have a huge marketing budget or sales force, he's going to be willing to pay out much more to get some help selling his product. He might pay out 50% or more!

There are lots of places where you can find affiliate marketing programs to join. Just Google "Affiliate Marketing" and you'll find a ton.

Some of the more popular sites are CommissionJunction.com and ClickBank.com and those sites tend to list smaller merchants.

Many major companies offer affiliate programs too, like Amazon.com and eBay.com

When you get right down to it, you can find an affiliate program for just about any type of product you want to sell.

Basically it works like this: you sign up with the affiliate product and they will give you an affiliate marketing URL.

It'll look something like this:

www.theirsite.com/js23b4

Whenever someone goes to that website, it redirects to the page selling whatever product you're selling. The site will place a cookie in the web browser of everyone who visits that URL. The cookie is a bit of tracking code that allows the company to keep track of the people who came from your specific URL. That way if they purchase the product now (or even later) you'll get credit for it.

Your job is to funnel as many people to that URL as possible.

Where most people fail with Affiliate Marketing is by not treating it as an actual business.

They think they can just buy a bunch of ads and point those ads to their affiliate marketing URL. As long as they spend less on the ads than they earn in commissions, they win.

In theory that might work...but it takes an incredibly sophisticated ad buyer to thread that needle.

Instead, I suggest you build your own website, as if the product was your own. Then direct the "order now" buttons to your affiliate marketing URL.

That's what I did when I was into affiliate marketing a few years back and I made a ton of money.

When I say "build a website like the product is your own", I mean it. You should even try to collect the email addresses of your site visitors so that you can do email marketing to them in the future.

Let's take an example. Let's say you want to sell treadmills; so you go to Amazon and sign up for their affiliate program.

Now you can build a website about the specific treadmills you want to sell off of Amazon.

On that website, write articles about each treadmill describing their benefits.

Write an eBook comparing the ten best treadmills and give it away on your website in exchange for people signing up for your treadmill newsletter.

Create a walking club membership section of your site where members can post their longest walking times and compete for prizes against each other.

Whatever.

Treat it like your own business, build stuff around it, create a community of people who are interested in treadmills and exercise.

Then on every article you write, on every blog post you create, on every social media post you launch, put an "Order now" button that points to your Amazon.com affiliate checkout page for that specific treadmill.

People won't think it's weird at all to be on your website one minute and be on Amazon checking out the next. Just put a little disclaimer next to the order link saying something like "all orders processed through Amazon.com for your safety" or some shit like that.

Do you get the idea?

If you build your own website, you have some measure of control. That's incredibly important because Amazon might stop selling the specific brand of treadmill that you're pushing. If that happens you're screwed…but not if you own your own website and control your email lists!

Because if Amazon suddenly stops selling that treadmill, you can run out and find another affiliate program somewhere else that does sell that treadmill (maybe one of the major sports gear websites like

SportsAuthority.com –well, I guess they just went out of business – but you get the idea).

Once you find another affiliate program selling that product, you can just update the links on your website to point towards that new affiliate URL.

Crisis averted.

The point being, affiliate marketing is great but leaves you without control...*unless* you take control by building your own website around the affiliate marketing program.

And most Affiliate Marketing programs are totally fine with this. Hell, most of them will even give you pictures of the products that you can use on your own website. They don't care, they want you to sell as many of their products as possible and that makes it a win win for everyone.

So if you're looking to just ease into this whole dot com thing, affiliate marketing may be just the thing for you.

Things To Keep In Mind

What sort of product should you sell? The same rules apply as earlier. It should be something that you can identify the market for and easily target. It should be something that a group of people are clamoring for.

All things being equal, I like to sell affiliate products that are higher priced.

Why sell something from Amazon.com that retails for $19 (when you might only earn 3% or

$.57 cents per sale) when you can just as easily sell something that retails for $149 (which at 3% would earn you $4.47 per sale)?

I know what you're thinking right now....$.57 cents or $4.47, neither of them is a lot of money.

Well, you're right. But that's the tradeoff. You don't have to spend the money to build the initial product. You don't have to spend the money to deal with customer support, or shipping, or inventory, or insurance, or any of the many other costs of creating your own product.

It's stress free. You just send the customers over and collect your commission.

And it might not be a lot of money, but if you can get good at marketing, and sell dozens or even hundreds of items per day; the money can add up.

I like to recommend Affiliate Marketing for people just getting started because it allows them to dip their toe in the water without a big upfront investment. It teaches you to build a simple website, and it teaches you how to generate traffic through Internet marketing.

Then once you get those fundamentals down, you can branch out and build your own product... or learn to become a sophisticated affiliate marketer and scale the business out to generate serious cash. But that's a topic for another book.

CHAPTER EIGHT

***

ADVERTISING BASED CONTENT CREATION

Another business model is the Advertising based content creation model. A lot of newbies like this model because it can potentially be done with little startup money and it seems sexy and fun. The reality is much different, as we'll see.

So what is this? Basically with this business model you create content, all kinds of content, and you attract site visitors to that content; lots of them. Then you sell advertising space on your site.

That's it pretty much it.

Whatever you can earn in advertising is what you earn in this model.

If you're particularly clever, you might sprinkle in some affiliate marketing type products into the mix to create a second income stream off your content, but that's not always possible.

So what am I talking about when I say "content"?

Content can be anything that you create; it can be blog posts or articles that you write, it can be a podcast, it can be an ongoing video series or weekly newsletter of some sort. Content is anything you can create and put out there that attracts eyeballs; which can then be sold to advertisers.

You've probably seen the kids with their youtube channels about makeup with 15 million subscribers. These kids are pulling in hundreds of thousands of dollars.

You've probably also read numerous blogs where the owners are making tons of money off advertising.

Or you've listened to podcasts with large followings (though granted, podcasts seem to be a little harder to monetize).

The point is; it's all about content.

A lot of those businesses focus on entertainment, but an advertising based content creation company doesn't have to be entertainment based.

I once owned a website called **EspressoShack.com** go check it out, it's still there in pretty much the same form (I milked the site for all it was worth and when the ad revenue started to decline I sold the site for a nice chunk of change).

That site is about espresso machines and coffee machines, and various other related things (coffee beans, coffee machine accessories, etc). The site is purely a content website designed to grab SEO traffic and sell ad space.

It's basically a site with tons of articles I wrote about different espresso machines. I compared different models, discussed features, talked about prices, and all kinds of stuff like that.

It's not entertainment; it's information-based education for someone interested in buying an espresso machine.

Let's face it... espresso machines are kind of complicated and expensive. People need guidance, and that's where my site came in.

If memory serves, I wrote around a hundred different articles on the site. You'll notice that many of the articles have links in them where you can purchase the specific espresso machine that I'm describing in the article. The links all point to Amazon.com and guess what; they were all affiliate links. So if someone clicked a link after reading my article and bought the espresso machine, I got a commission from Amazon. These days you have to disclose that those links are affiliate links (they passed some consumer protection law), but back then you didn't. It doesn't matter; you can easily put a small print disclaimer at the bottom of each page.

The site got a lot of good free traffic from Google because my articles were well written and informative.

The thing about building a content based ad business...you have to create good content. And that's hard to do, and takes time.

You also have to create *consistent* good content. My espresso site had over a hundred well researched and well written articles but today with all the competition out there, you'd probably need much more than that.

My espresso site used articles as the content vehicle. These days, and into the future, <u>it's all about video</u>.

I recommend that you build your own site and post your videos there, but then also spray them all over the place as well. Create your own Youtube channel and post your videos there, post them on Vimeo and other video hosting sites; post them wherever you can. The more eyeballs you can gather, the more ad space you can sell.

It's a hard business. Content creation is tough, and doing it consistently for months before you see results is hard to do. Why does it take so long? Building up an audience just takes a while. It's hard to build content AND market that content at the same time.

SELLING ADVERTISING

How do you sell advertising? It's really very easy. When you start out you're going to use Google Adsense, that's the flip side of Google's Adwords program.

Adsense allows anyone to sell ads on their site without having to actually sell ads; Google takes care of that for you. They'll give you a little snippet of code that you put on each page of your website. That code will scan each page and determine on its own what kind of content you have and what sort of advertisements should be shown.

You have some little control over this, but not really. You can suggest preferences over on your Adsense account, but by and large Google will determine this all on their own using their magic algorithms.

Adsense is a pay per click platform; that means you only earn money if someone clicks on an ad.

This is a tricky needle to thread! You want your site visitors to click the ads, but if they do that then they leave your site. On the other hand, if your content is so interesting that they don't notice the ads; well, you won't make any money!

Google also places restrictions

on how many ads you can place on each page (three last I checked) and where you can put those ads. They're picky too; break their guidelines and they'll kick you right out of the program. They aren't messing around!

As time goes on and you build your brand and refine your target market, you may be able to move away from Google Adsense. Adsense is great when you're starting out, but you'll likely be able to make more money selling ad space directly to companies.

What companies? That's for you to know. In fact, you should build each content website with the idea, from day one, of which types of companies you would eventually like to sell ad space to. This will determine the type of content you create.

Someone hosting a weekly video series that teaches young girls how to apply makeup is going to sell ad space to a makeup company, not a bowling ball company...right? So keep all these constituencies in mind when creating your site.

Ask yourself who the content is targeted to, and what types of products would those people like to buy.

Everything you produce should be focused on those two things.

CONTENT CALENDAR

Whenever you build this type of site, it's important to create a content calendar; which is basically a calendar with the different content you plan to create mapped out into the future. Whatever your production schedule is (it might be daily, it might be weekly, it might be monthly if you really want to push your luck) you need to map out the different content pieces you plan to create as far into the future as possible...and then stick to that schedule.

It's a good idea to produce as much content into the future all at once as you can. So if you plan on releasing a new video every Friday, record four or five or six of them in advance and have them ready to release beforehand.

Why? Well, shit happens. Life happens. You want to create a consistent flow of content, so people can come to count on it.

Skip days and you'll lose viewers. And believe me, you'll skip days. Something always happens. You get sick and can't create Friday's video. Your dog gets hit by a car and you get depressed and go on a drinking binge for a week. You're girlfriend/boyfriend/wife/husband leaves you and you fall into a funk.

Whatever. If you've created a half dozen videos (or articles or blog posts or podcasts or whatever) then you can continue on schedule without any problems.

A content calendar allows you to do this and helps you craft the message you're trying to create.

It's important to treat these content websites the same as you would a product website. In this case, the "product" is the content and the eyeballs it generates.

Do the same things you would do with a product website; things like collect site visitors email addresses so you can send them a series of follow up emails to keep them coming back to the site.

Once you build an email list, you have a built in audience that you can call on in the future. It allows you to announce every time you release new content for an immediate bump in traffic. It also allows you to market affiliate products to them in the future.

Hell, you can even put ads in the emails that you send out.

Mind = blown.

When you get right down to it, email marketing is the cornerstone of every single successful business online no matter what kind of business it is. I probably said that earlier and I'll keep saying it.

Listen, content related ad based businesses are very hard to build, but they can be a lot of fun...even if they aren't entertainment related.

My espresso website was a lot of fun to build; mostly because I love espresso, but are because there are all kinds of benefits to reap. Once I built an audience, I could have gotten all the major espresso companies to send me free espresso machines so that I could more deeply review them. Companies love to send out product to bloggers and vloggers.

Of course, these days you have to disclose to your readers or viewers that you were given the item for free in exchange for a review. But that's no big deal.

The main thing I want to leave you with when it comes to these types of businesses is that it takes an enormous amount of time and effort to do it right. Months.

Creating content is hard. Creating high quality content is even harder. Creating high quality content day after day after day for month after month after month is excruciatingly hard.

But it can be a lot of fun too.

CHAPTER NINE

***

ECOMMERCE

Finally, I want to talk briefly about ecommerce. This is the last of the five business models that I mentioned earlier, and to be honest; I only mentioned it in the interest of being as complete as possible.

When you get right down to it, ecommerce is not something that many people reading this book should get into; at least not unless and until you have a great deal more experience.

When I hear ecommerce, I think of sites like Amazon, or eBay; huge websites selling lots of different products.

Sure, you don't have to build the next Amazon.com to get into ecommerce, you can focus on any one of an infinite number of small niches.

You could run a golf supply

website, or a treadmill website, or a bow hunting website, or a knitting needle website. Those are all examples of ecommerce.

The problem is, you're going to need to either manufacture many products yourself, or order bulk manufactured products from somewhere like China where you can get a good deal by bulk.

There are websites like Alibaba.com that will hook you up with manufacturers of all types; but you'll need to order in bulk from them.

And then you'll need to warehouse your inventory, and deal with shipping and support and all the things.

In a word…it's a hassle. In two words…it's an *expensive hassle*. In three words…it's a *risky expensive hassle.* You get the idea.

IT really doesn't lend itself to the whole concept of living a dot com lifestyle! But it does work if you do it right. A lot of people are making a lot of money doing this sort of thing. I mean millions.

It just takes a lot of expertise and a lot of luck. And really, who needs that sort of hassle?

On the flip side, I really like the idea of creating faux (fake) ecommerce sites like I talked about in the last chapter.

My example of a treadmill site selling lots of different brands of treadmills through the Amazon affiliate program is basically an ecommerce site... you just don't have to deal with all the hassle of regular ecommerce sites since

Amazon will be fulfilling all the orders for you.

I've built thousands of sites just like that in the past and had a great deal of fun doing it. If you absolutely have to get into ecommerce, I recommend going with the fake ecommerce site!

That's all I'm going to talk about ecommerce. It's really such a complicated thing that it would take an entire book, and I'm not an expert in it.

If you're interested in building fake ecommerce sites though, well I am a bit of an expert in that. I built a couple video courses over at Codemy.com that walks you through it. The main one is called

"Thin Affiliate Niche Websites With PHP"

www.codemy.com/thin

And the other is called:

"PHP Programming For Affiliate Marketers"

www.codemy.com/affiliate

They're both worth a watch if you're into all this affiliate marketing stuff, especially at scale (though the second one is more about coding in the PHP programming language than it is about affiliate marketing).

Either way, if you feel the urge to plunge into real ecommerce, resist that urge! If you must, dip your toe in the water with fake ecommerce and go from there!

CHAPTER TEN

***

BUILDING WEBSITES

So let's talk about building things, specifically websites and some of the things that go along with them.

I can't teach you how to build a website in one chapter, but I can point you in the right direction, and explain a few things that go along with it that you're going to need to know.

The good news is; it's never been easier to build a website. There are tons of tools out there, most free, that will allow you to create a pretty damn good looking website with little to no computer programming or web development skills.

And we're not talking about building the next Facebook or Twitter here. You'd need some mad skills to do something like that and if you're reading this book; chances are you don't have those skills and you're not going to learn them in a book.

No, we're just talking about building basic business websites that will showcase whatever product you're selling and allow people to purchase it.

It's a lot easier than you might think to build something like that.

I'm going to nudge you towards Wordpress; it's not just blog software anymore. These days you can create some pretty sophisticated websites with Wordpress, all without needing to know anything at all about web development.

Wordpress comes pre-installed on most basic web hosting packages (we'll talk about web hosting in a bit), or if not; it's easily installed.

And with Wordpress, you have tons of options when it comes to the look and feel of your site as well as the functionality.

Wordpress is built around the concept of "themes" and "plugins". Themes deal with the look of the site, and plugins deal with the functionality.

Installing both themes and plugins is done in a point and click manner, there's no programming experience required.

Basically, once Wordpress is installed, you log into your Wordpress dashboard. From there you can change themes, install and deploy plugins, add and modify pages of the site, and other stuff.

I made a Wordpress video course over at Codemy.com if you want to learn step by step how to create Wordpress sites. It's pretty simple once you see it done once. The course is regularly $47 but use coupon code "**dotcom**" at checkout (all one word without quotes); I'll give you the course for <u>free</u>. Check it out at **Codemy.com/wordpress**

Why free? Because! Building a website is incredibly important for living the dot com lifestyle, and I wanted to give you solid step by step information in this book, not just theory and pretty bullshit. Unfortunately there isn't room here to teach you everything about Wordpress in one chapter, and it would be much easier for me to show you using video than to write it out in this book.

My Wordpress course is pretty short, just eight videos and an hour and a half long. Check it out!

DOMAIN NAMES

Whenever you build a website, you're going to want your own domain name. I'm talking about www.yourname.com

Domain names are kind of weird in that you don't actually own them, you rent them yearly. I guess you own the right to continue renting it (if you want to look at it that way).

Domain names generally cost around $10 a year depending on where you purchase them. You purchase a domain name from something called a "registrar" and there are tons of different registrars out there.

Godaddy.com is a popular domain name registrar and you've probably seen their annoying commercials all over television. Godaddy probably has the cheapest prices for a new registration because they often run sales, but then they do all sorts of slimy things like jack up the price for later years or try to upsell you a bunch of nonsense products that you don't need. I'd stay away from them.

The registrar I use is called **NameCheap.com** and they have just about the lowest prices I've found, while at the same time being a company with integrity that doesn't yank you around like a lot of other registrars do.

I highly recommend them.

There are lots of different types of domain names these days; I'm talking .com, .net, .org, .co, .info, .whatever.

For your purposes, you should

always stick with a .com domain name. That is sometimes easier said than done. Believe me; the domain name you want is probably already taken. You'll have to get creative.

For instance, if you plan to sell golf clubs, you might want to register golfclubs.com

Of course, that domain name is taken. So you might try:

➢ DiscountGolfClubs.com

➢ MyGolfClubs.com

➢ BuyGolfClubs.com

➢ eGolfClubs.com

…or some other variation. It can be incredibly frustrating, and that's why people settle for other types of domain names besides .com (like .net or .org), or they use hyphens in the name (like golf-clubs.com).

I recommend that you don't do any of those things if possible. Most people expect .com domains; anything else seems unprofessional or confusing.

I always register my domain names for just the minimum one year. Then when that year is up, I renew it for another year. Don't worry, your registrar will email you when the year is nearly up and remind you to renew it (or you can set it up to auto-renew).

But if you don't renew it and pay the fee, you'll lose the domain name. Because of that, some people choose to register their domain names for multiple years, like five or ten years. There's nothing wrong with that, you just have to pay all at once. So if the registrar you choose charges $9.57 cents per year and you choose to register it for ten years, you'll pay $95.70, which isn't all that expensive when you get right down to it.

You can also purchase domain names on the secondary market, ie from people who currently "own" them. Even though people are technically just renting them, they can still sell their domain names to someone else, or buy one from someone who already owns it.

There are websites that specialize in that like sedo.com and flippa.com but be advised, a domain name can be sold for any amount of money the owner chooses. It might have only cost them $10 bucks to register it, but that owner can turn around and sell it for $50,000 if they want, or more. The price is solely determined by how much someone is willing to pay for it.

I've seen domain names sold for millions of dollars. Insurance.com was sold for $35.6 million bucks. Sex.com sold for $14 million bucks. Hotels.com sold for $11 million bucks...and my favorite, Whisky.com sold for $3.1 million.

The business of domain flipping is big business. I've bought domain names from people on the secondary market. I bought the domain name for my current site, Codemy.com from someone for an arm and a leg. I bought MarketingFool.com from someone off of Sedo.com and I recently bought ComeVisit.org on the secondary market (I plan on building a travel website on it).

Whenever you buy a domain name on the secondary market, you're going to pay more...much more. Sometimes it might be worth it...most times it won't. Very few people type a domain name into their web browser. Most people see a link to the site somewhere and click the link, in which case, the domain name doesn't really matter at all.

When you purchase a domain name, you then need to point it to wherever your website is hosted using something called a nameserver address (your specific registrar and web host will have instructions on how to do that).

But that begs the question; what

is a webhost and where does it fit into this whole thing?

WEB HOSTING

A web host is the place where your website sits. A website is a bunch of .html files, and those files need to sit on a web server somewhere so that people can access them. That's a webhost.

There are many many many webhosting solutions out there and the type of webhost you choose, as well as the cost, will be determined in large part by the type of website you'll be creating and the amount of traffic you think it will receive.

The more traffic your website gets, the more expensive your webhosting is going to be. It's a matter of bandwidth.

Think of it like your mobile phone plan. You get x gigs of data per month (like 6 gigs, or whatever). If you stream lots of movies on your phone, you're going to eat through those gigs and have to purchase more. It's the same with webhosting. You get a certain limit on bandwidth, and the more people that visit your site, the more bandwidth you use.

Luckily, the types of basic websites that you're going to be building don't require expensive webhosting and very little bandwidth; at least in the beginning. You only pay more if more people come to your site; and if more people come to your site it hopefully means that you're earning more money and can more easily afford to pay higher web hosting costs.

Webhosting breaks down into a couple of categories. There's cloud hosting solutions (like Amazon AWS, or Microsoft's Azure platform), and there's more basic traditional managed hosting.

Cloud hosting like AWS or Azure are always going to be more expensive and harder to deal with. With those solutions, you need MASSIVE technical experience because you have to do all the work yourself. You have to know how to deploy an actual web server, how to provision it, how to secure it from hackers...everything.

Cloud hosting is best left to the pros and the large scale companies who have entire teams of devop engineers who can handle all that stuff and the budgets to pay the hundreds to thousands of dollars per month that those things cost.

The option you're going to want to use is the more traditional managed hosting solutions.

In managed hosting all the behind the scenes things are taken care of for you. You don't need to know how to run a web server, or anything of the sort.

Most managed solutions have point and click user interfaces that will let you do the few things that you do need to do.

If you plan to use Wordpress, it becomes even easier.

One popular managed webhosting company that's been around forever is Hostgator.

I generally use more expensive cloud web hosting for my stuff, but I do use Hostgator for a few of my more simple websites. Frankly I'm not thrilled with the performance or their tech support, but for the price and what they offer it's a pretty good deal for someone just starting out.

Prices range from less than $10 dollars per month on up depending on how much traffic you think you'll get.

When it comes to managed web hosting, no matter which company you choose, you'll need to know a few things in order to choose the solution that's best for you. The big thing you'll need to understand is the concept of VPS, Dedicated Servers, and Shared Hosting.

SHARED HOSTING

I'll try not to geek out here too

much, but we need to discuss some tech concepts.

Websites run on web servers. Web servers are just like regular computers, but hooked up to the backbone of the Internet. Those web hosting companies run huge warehouses full of those computers all running 24/7.

The thing is, computers are expensive and you don't want to have to buy one of those servers to host a simple website.

So someone came up with the idea of virtualization, which allows them to take one server, and chop it up into dozens or hundreds of virtual servers all sitting on the same physical machine.

The web hosting company can then rent out space on that machine to dozens or hundreds of websites.

They call this "Shared Hosting" because your website is sharing space on one physical computer in the warehouse.

So if it would normally costs you $500 to host your site alone on one computer, they can chop that computer into 10 mini-servers and everyone pays $50 a month each (10 x 50 = 500) and everyone is happy.

Sounds pretty good, right?

Well it is…if you're a small site and not a lot of people are going to be visiting your site. That's why shared managed hosting is so cheap.

The problem is, the web hosting company won't stop at 10 sites per machine; they'll cram as many people onto each machine as it will handle.   Dozens, sometimes hundreds of websites can get shoved onto one physical machine. And then performance starts to drag and your website seems laggy to people who are visiting it. It takes a long time for your page to load; or the whole site just "times out" and stays blank.

It happens.

But that's not so bad, because it's a tradeoff. It's super cheap and allows you to get your site up and running quickly and easily, but it might start to feel laggy if you start getting more traffic.

But if you start getting more traffic, you can upgrade to less and less shared levels of hosting.

VPS HOSTING

VPS stands for Virtual Private Server, and is basically just the name for splitting that web server we just talked about into dozens of small servers, virtually.

You mostly won't need to know anything about this because you probably won't be rooting around in your actual server. You'll use the web hosting companies graphical user interface to interact with your account (often called cpanel); or you'll be using Wordpress like I suggested and then you'll just use the Wordpress dashboard to make all the changes to your website.

Still, I thought you should learn the term because it will come up when choosing webhosting solutions and I thought you might like to at least know what it refers to.

DEDICATED SERVERS

Finally, a dedicated server is just the computer sitting in the warehouse at the web hosting company like we talked about before...there just aren't any other people using it. It is DEDICATED to you and you alone.

You're only probably ever going to need a dedicated server if your site has thousands of visitors hitting it all at the same time.

Dedicated servers are expensive, you can expect to pay anywhere from $100 bucks a month on up, depending on how much bandwidth you might need. It always seems to cost a few hundred bucks a month or more to run a dedicated server.

Dedicated servers can be

managed or not. You'll want managed and that will cost more.

If they aren't managed, then you'll be responsible for setting up the server, provisioning it with all the crap it needs to run correctly, securing it against hackers, and on and on. You don't want any part of that because it's simply not something you can do without advanced training or a computer science degree.

THE BOTTOM LINE

The bottom line is this; start out with a cheap shared hosting account or shared VPS account at a company like hostgator.com or one of the dozens of similar companies out there (you can search Google for webhosting and get a ton of results).

Then, as your business grows and more people visit your site each day, you can slowly bump up to the more expensive shared solutions, and then the more expensive VPS solutions, until finally one day you may need a dedicated server.

Upgrading is usually a point and click thing, or if not; the web hosting company will take care of it all for you.

OTHER WEBSITE THINGS

What other things do we need to think about when it comes to building a website?

The first thing that comes to mind is analytics; or tracking data. You need to be able to tell how many people are coming to your website, how long they're sticking around, and exactly what they're doing while they are there.

I use Google Analytics for all my basic website analytics. It's totally free and incredibly robust. There are other tools out there that cost money and might give you more data (and more specific data), but for free, Google Analytics gives you everything you'll need when you're just starting out.

Head over to their website: Google.com/analytics and sign up for a free account.

To use it, they'll give you a snippet of javascript code that you need to put at the bottom of every page of your website. If you're using Wordpress, most "themes" will handle this for you. Just log into your Wordpress dashboard and look through your theme settings. There's probably a box where you can paste that snippet of javascript code and save it. Then Wordpress will take care of the rest and automatically put that code at the bottom of every page of your site.

It's so important to install analytics on your site right away so that you have complete data from day one. These days it's all about big data and analytics. You'll need to get into the habit of pouring over your data daily. It'll help you understand your customers and how they interact with your site.

You might find out that 89% of site visitors leave your site after visiting a certain page. Why? Well, you'll look into it and try to figure that out. You'll make changes to that page and then watch the analytics. Do people still leave? Tweak more. You get the idea.

Google has tutorials that will teach you the basic functionality of their Analytics program, and you'll need to read them to learn how to use it. There are also probably books on the subject and other tutorials and blog posts about it. It's worth your time to become as expert on this stuff as possible.

EMAIL MARKETING

I know I've already mentioned how important email marketing is and I just can't stress it enough; but how do you actually integrate email marketing into your website?

In the past I used a company

called aWeber.com to handle all my email marketing, but then MailChimp came along and blew them out of the water...now I use MailChimp for everything and I recommend them to everyone.

Just head over to their website: MailChimp.com and sign up for a free account. You only pay as more and more people join your email list.

To integrate MailChimp into your website, they'll give you a snippet of javascript code (similar to what Google Analytics did) that you need to place on your website wherever you want a form to appear that gives your site visitors the chance to join your email list.

Further, there are tons of MailChimp plugins that you can add to your Wordpress website that will automate the whole thing.

For instance, if your Wordpress site also handles order processing, there are probably plugins that will add the email addresses of your customers to your email list whenever they order something.

The point is, it's pretty easy to integrate your email marketing into your website using third party products like MailChimp.

CHAPTER ELEVEN

✳✳✳

MARKETING AND MONEY

Ok, so you've decided on a basic business model. Hopefully you're either building some sort of digital product, or you've picked some sort of affiliate product and built yourself a website and you're ready to go.

Now what?

From here on out there are two things you'll need to focus on every single day. These will be the cornerstone of your existence from here on out. What are these mysterious things?

Traffic and Conversion

Yes the two most important things to any web business owner are traffic and conversion. Or to put it another way: getting people to your website, and converting them into paying customers.

They're both critically important and it's not enough to focus on one or the other of them; you need both.

You could have a million people visiting your website every single day, but if they aren't converting; if they aren't buying your stuff, then that traffic is useless.

On the other hand, you can craft your website copy beautifully in a way that makes people BEG YOU to buy your stuff...but if no one ever visits your site, if you have no site traffic; you're screwed.

Traffic and conversion, they're the end-all and be-all of your existence.

Getting people to your website is hard, damn hard. Converting those people into buyers is even harder. You need to fire on all cylinders to get this right. Each requires a specific set of skills. Learn those skills and the world is yours. Fail to learn them, and you're done.

CONVERSION

So let's talk about conversion first. Traffic is a little easier; conversion is where the magic really happens.

I'm going to teach you a new word that you probably aren't familiar with (or you've heard it before in different context). The word is; *copywriting*.

When most people hear that word, they think of that little symbol that they see all over the place; ©. You see it in books, at the bottom of websites; basically anywhere some bit of text is legally protected. "Copyright © 2016 All Rights Reserved".

That's not the type of copywriting I'm talking about. I'm talking about the art and science of <u>writing copy</u>.

Copy is text, usually in print (like a newspaper or magazine – and now the web) and usually related to advertising.

You might have heard the term "ad copy".

Basically copywriting is the act of convincing someone to do something through text.

Have I confused you yet?

Let me ask you this… What are you trying to do with your website? You're trying to convince someone to do something. The thing you're trying to convince them to do is buy something from you. How are you trying to convince them? You're convincing them through the text or images or video on your website.

That text, or images, or video is "copywriting" and there's an art and a science to it.

Since the beginning of the written word, people have been convincing people to do things with words. Magazines have ads in them, newspapers have ads in them, television has ads on them. Even though television is visual, someone had to write the copy for the ad – the script for the commercial. It's all words that convince people to do things. It's all copywriting.

You need to learn copywriting because while it is an art, there's also a lot of science involved and there are specific rules that you need to follow; formats that will help you; techniques to use; and things to avoid.

I learned copywriting by studying the old masters from decades in the past. Back in the old day before television, everything was sold via ads in newspapers and magazines. The people that crafted those ads laid the foundation for the modern copywriting industry and we still follow the rules they created today.

After all, the web is really just a fancy newspaper or magazine with video and user interactions. The principles of convincing people to buy stuff haven't really changed. Human psychology hasn't really changed.

Some of those "old masters" of

copywriting are:

- ➢ Claude Hopkins

- ➢ Robert Collier

- ➢ John Caples

- ➢ David Ogilvy

- ➢ Lester Wunderman

Those guys set the foundation for everything we know about copywriting, and they all wrote books teaching you their methods. Those books are amazing; and priceless...though oddly enough you can find them on Amazon for next to nothing ($10 bucks or less).

Some of them are even free online if you just look around a bit.

Check out Claude Hopkins two book set: "My Life in Advertising & Scientific Advertising" available on Kindle for $9.99

You get two books in one. Scientific Advertising is dry; it feels sort of like a textbook, whereas My Life In Advertising teaches you his methods in a more story-telling approach. They're both great starts.

Next I recommend you check out Robert Colliers book: "The Robert Collier Letterbook". You can find the Kindle version of this one for $5.99 and the used hardcover for less than $10 bucks. That book is old, very old…but amazing.

Finally, check out John Caples book: "Tested Advertising Methods (5th Edition)". I think that book is out of print but you can get it used on Amazon for less than $5 bucks.

Those books will teach you copywriting in a way I couldn't hope to in this book and I highly recommend you check them out.

There are a few modern masters that I follow as well, people like:

> Joseph Sugarman (remember those cheesy blu-blocker sunglass commercials years and years ago? That was him)

> Bob Bly

> Dan Kennedy

They've all written books on

copywriting and all have blogs that you can check out for free. I suggest you do some Google searching and check them out.

Back in the day, the medium was different (newspapers and magazines verses websites), but the principles are the same.

Back then you had a headline, followed by body copy, followed by a call to action. Today it's much the same way. Websites have some sort of attention grabbing headline at the top of them, or maybe it's an image, or maybe it's a video. The principle of grabbing people attention right at the top of the page is the same though.

Your website will then have body copy, in the form of text or video explaining what you are selling, whetting the customer's appetite, making them want the thing you're selling.

Finally your site will have some sort of call to action; "click here to order now" or something like that. It's all just copywriting and you need to learn how to do it correctly or you will fail.

And believe me when I tell you that you can't guess with this stuff. You can't "wing it". You can't be like: "oh I'll just try it this way", no. You have to follow the rules of copywriting that have worked forever. Human psychology hasn't changed. You need to learn the buttons to push in order to make someone want to buy your crap.

Start with Hopkins "My Life in Advertising"; read it. Then read the Robert Collier Letter book, then Caples Tested Advertising

Methods.

Check out other websites. See how they're using those principles and techniques that you'll learn in those books. You'll notice that everyone is using those techniques in some way.

You'll build what are called "Landing Pages" on your website. Those are pages off of your main homepage that you'll direct new visitors to (through some of the traffic generating techniques we'll talk about in a minute).

You'll learn to test those landing pages, tweak them, change little things about them and watch to see if your conversion rates go up or down. You'll change things like the headline of the page, or the colors, or the images used.

You'll find that you'll always be

testing and tweaking your landing pages to get the best conversion. Conversion rates are always low. Only 2-3% of all people that visit your webpage will convert; less than that if the page is a hard sell.

Making a tiny change that bumps that up to 4% results in big money for you. You'll spend a lot of time on this, perhaps becoming obsessed. There are tons of tools out there that help you test landing pages. You can Google it.

The most successful people don't just "hard sell" their stuff. They create chains. The first step in the chain is to collect the email address of your site visitor in exchange for giving them something free. Then you set up a series of automated follow-up emails that both educate and sell over time. This is where your email marketing comes into place. Email marketing is all just copywriting too.

Most people won't buy stuff from you right away (or from anyone right away). The old adage is that it takes a person seven times interacting with you (reading your emails, seeing your ads, whatever) before they will buy. I've found that to be more or less true over the years.

That's why it's so important to get their email address right away and then chip away at them over time.

TRAFFIC

Traffic is a little bit easier to wrap your head around. You can always just buy traffic from Google in the form of Adwords advertising.

Adwords is great because you only pay per click, meaning it only costs you money if a person visits your site. The problem with Adwords is that it can be incredibly expensive, even if you know what you're doing (and massively so if you don't know what you're doing).

Remember when we talked about the lifetime value of a customer? If you know, generally speaking, that each customer is going to spend around a hundred dollars with you, then you can spend up to a hundred dollars on advertising to bring that person to your site and still make a profit. This is a gross over-simplification, but you get the idea.

Google Pay Per Click (PPC)

advertising is great if you know the conversion rates of your website. Let's say that you know that out of every 800 people who visit your site, 1 person will buy something from you for $39 bucks. How much can you spend on advertising to bring those 800 people to your site and still break even?

Well, $39 divided by 800 is $.05 cents. So you can tell Google that you're willing to pay 5 cents per click.

The problem is, Google Adwords is an auction based system, meaning that other people are also bidding on those same clicks. Someone else might be willing to pay 10 cents per click (because their site converts better or any number of other reasons). They'll get the traffic; you won't because they're willing to pay more.

But I'm getting off on a tangent here. I don't recommend you dive right in and start spending ad money as a newbie.

I talked earlier about picking a product that already has a group of people clamoring for it. If you do that, then you don't necessarily have to spend money on advertising in the traditional way. Instead you can focus on Growth Hacking for your traffic (at least initially).

GROWTH HACKING

Growth Hacking is the cool new term for Internet marketing, but it's not really new. It's really been around forever. Back in the day we just used to call it "Guerilla

Marketing". Growth Hacking just sounds more hip - more web 2.0.

Growth Hacking is the art and science of getting people to your website without spending money to do it.

There are infinite ways to Growth Hack, and each method needs to be tailored to your specific product and industry.

That is to say, a Growth Hacking method that worked for one company, may not work for you. This makes it kind of hard to *teach* growth hacking. But here goes anyway...

I'll start by giving you a couple of growth hacking strategies that worked in the past for others (one from a notable company, the other from my own experience).

Do you remember Hotmail? It

was one of the first web based email providers (way before Gmail). A couple of guys built it without much venture capital money. If memory serves, I believe that they only raised a few hundred thousand dollars.

In the venture capital world, three hundred grand is mere peanuts. These days, idiot kids with idiot business ideas routinely raise millions in VC money, but Hotmail came out in the late 90's and things were a little different back then.

Basically, these guys simply didn't have the money to spend on traditional advertising and their product wasn't catching on by word of mouth like they hoped it would.

So someone came up with this growth hacking idea; put a small text advertisement at the bottom of every single email that went out across their platform. The text said: "PS, I love you, Get Your Free Email At Hotmail.com".

They quickly removed the "PS I love you part" and kept the "Get Your Free Email At Hotmail.com" part.

What happened? Before they tried this, they had gotten about 20,000 people a month to sign up. After they started adding that snippet of text to all the emails that people sent, user signups exploded.

The very next month, 1 million new users signed up. Less than a year later between 9 and 12 MILLION people had signed up (remember back then there were only about 70 million people online so 12 million is a HUGE percentage). At the end of that year the two founders sold the company to Microsoft for $400 Million dollars.

All from adding that small line of text to all outgoing email sent through their platform.

That's Growth Hacking. It's about using your own systems to sell for you. It's about creating a situation where viral marketing can happen organically. It's about getting other people to spread the word for you. It's basically just Guerilla Marketing.

Back in the late 90's I created one of the Internet's first advertising network websites. It was called BannerClicks. Catchy no? If you owned a website, you could sign up for BannerClicks and get a little snippet of computer code to put on your website. That snippet of code would show banner ads on your site, and keep track of how many impressions were served and how many people clicked on each ad.

The Growth Hacking bit came next. I set the system up so that for every two ads you showed on your websites, you would receive a credit that would allow you to show one of YOUR ads on someone else's website.

Thinking back, the whole thing seems a little bit like a pyramid scheme, but it worked.

Traffic to your site generated credit that you could use to show your own ads on other people's sites, which in turn would bring new traffic to YOUR site, which would earn you credit and show your ads on still other sites, which would generate traffic, which would earn you credit, which would, which would, which would...

You get the idea. The whole thing fed off itself and self-generated traffic and ads.

Sure, as a member you benefitted; but since the system was set up on a 2:1 ratio (for every 2 ads shown on your site, you got 1 credit), the real winner was *me* because you were generating ad views (2:1) that I could sell to other advertisers. The house always wins.

Anyway, this bit of Growth Hacking propelled my ad network into immediate growth and in the first three months we had shown over a million ads across the network.

A million doesn't seem like much today, but back in the late 90's it was unheard of.

I sold that company to a publicly traded company at the height of the dot com stock market book of the late 90's early 2000's.

I didn't invest any money into the thing, I built it myself and the Growth Hacking took care of the rest.

So how can you Growth Hack your own site? Who knows!

You'll have to figure that out yourself. Will the growth hack that I used on my ad network or the one the Hotmail guys be useful to you? Nope.

You've got to figure out your own growth hack that plays to the strengths or weaknesses of your own product and target market.

Think about it from your customers' points of view. How can you build a system that encourages THEM to sell your stuff for you?

In both of my examples, the customers did all the selling (every time someone sent an email using Hotmail, they were inadvertently sending a Hotmail Ad, and every time someone came to the website of one of my ad network members they were inadvertently generating credits for the site owner that generated more traffic for them and more ad views for my network).

So figure out a way to make your own customers sell for you without even realizing they're doing it.

Sounds a little like voodoo. It is.

It's Growth Hacking, and if you get it right, the sky's the limit.

TRADITIONAL INTERNET MARKETING

Apart from Growth Hacking, there's a ton of traditional Internet Marketing techniques that you should use as well.

Search Engine Optimization (SEO) is one of the most popular forms of Internet Marketing that newbies focus on because they think it's free. The idea is that you get your site ranked well at Google and then you get a bunch of free traffic.

That's becoming less and less possible as Google tightens its grip on their search algorithm and seems to send traffic more and more to their own properties and less and less to small websites like yours and mine.

Still, there is some traffic to be gained from a good search ranking (if you can manage to get it). Just realize that it isn't free traffic. You have to spend *time* in order to get it, and time is worth even more than money – especially in a dot com lifestyle.

I'm not going to go into SEO in detail here, I've literally written whole books on the subject. I built one of the earliest and most popular SEO tools (the Submission-Spider) back in the late 90's (before there even WAS a Google), but I don't sell it anymore because the industry is so weird and Google controls it so tightly.

But you can do some research to

learn SEO on your own. There are tons of free tutorials out there.

Inbound marketing is popular these days. I can't figure out exactly what that is, but it has something to do with content marketing, writing blog posts, things like that. Google it if you're interested.

Joint ventures are also a popular form of Internet Marketing. In a JV, you find some other company or website and team up with them in some way to leverage their customer base. Maybe they have a product that compliments yours that their customers might want. So you team up and cut them in on the profits.

JV's are good for people who are just starting out because you can leverage someone else who is established. And generally they don't cost you anything up front. The hard part is finding a company to partner with and getting them to agree to do it. It's another strategy that takes time, not money.

Social Media marketing is another typical Internet Marketing technique that generally revolves around content creation and virality.

To be honest, I've never really spent much time with Social Media marketing. I've got a Facebook account that I use for personal stuff, and a Twitter account @flatplanet where I post business related stuff (are you following me?) but I don't put much actual effort into it. I guess I find that Growth Hacking is more interesting than Social Media marketing, but the rest of the world surely seems enamored with it.

I used to run a website called **MarketingFool.com**

Actually, I still own the site; I just haven't updated it in several years.

But I wrote a couple hundred blog posts and articles on different types of Internet Marketing and SEO stuff there. It's all free, though it might be a little outdated. Check it out if you're bored, or just head to Google and search for Internet Marketing and I'm sure you'll find tons of blogs and tutorials that you can read to learn the latest cool Internet Marketing techniques.

You'll always be learning this stuff, it never ends because there's always some new method out, some new guru teaching some new trick, or some latest greatest technique.

So Traffic and Conversion…the two cornerstones of living the dot com lifestyle.

Those are the toughest things to learn and they're the toughest things to get right; but if you can figure them out – there's not much you can't do in this world…

CHAPTER TWELVE

***

MARKET RESEARCH

I want to spend a few minutes talking about market research. How do you figure out if a particular product even has a market?

I've said before that the first thing is to know your customers and know how they behave and where they hang out online. There's probably some web forum, or Facebook page, or user group where they congregate.

But that isn't always possible, and you might not know your potential clients all that well. So how do you do market research?

These days there are tons of tools online that will give you all kinds of market research. Most of them cost money, some cost a lot of money.

You can do some Google

searches and find them, and then pay for them. But I'm going to show you a few of the free ones that I use. You can get a surprisingly lot of information from these free tools.

The first tool I use is the Google Keyword Tool. This used to be a standalone tool, but they've integrated it into the Google Adwords program. So to use it, you have to sign up for Adwords. Head over to Google.com/adwords and sign up.

You might have to give them a credit card to join, but you don't have to actually spend any money on that credit card to use the Keyword tool. Log in and look at the top of the screen and you should see a menu. Click the "Tools" link and then the "Keyword Planner" link.

What is it? Basically that tool lets you type in a keyword and it will give you Google search data on the keyword (ie it will tell you how many people searched for that keyword last month at Google). It will also give you different keyword suggestions based on the keyword that you entered.

It will also show you historic trends for the search data as well.

Not only that, but it will show you what people are paying, on average, to advertise on Google for those keywords. That is, it shows you what the average cost per click for those specific keywords are.

That's great information to know because it gives you an indication of how commercial that keyword is, as well as what kind of competition you might face if you go into that niche with a product of your own.

Another mind blowing feature allows you to type in the URL of any website, and the tool will analyze that site and tell you what Google thinks the keywords that relate to that website are. Wow!

If you poke around in there you can find all kinds of useful information. There are all sorts of filters you can use to narrow stuff down.

And for the price, free, you really just can't beat it.

Another useful free tool is the Google trends tool, which you can find at: google.com/trends

That thing shows you what's trending on Google at the moment, as well as what's trending on

Youtube. It breaks things down by category and by date. So you can find trends related to your product.

That tool is less about market research and more about what's going on at the moment, which is useful if you're doing any sort of blogging or content marketing and want to piggyback off of any current trending topics.

Play around with it, you'll find all kinds of useful information in there.

Another free tool that I like is the SpyFu.com keyword tool. It gives you all kinds of data on Google keywords that people are spending Adwords PPC money on.

You can enter a keyword and it will tell you the monthly searches locally and globally, the click through rate for that keyword, the cost per click to buy advertising for that keyword, and how many people are currently bidding on that keyword.

That last bit of information is particularly useful to help you gauge your potential competition.

Like the Google keyword tool, you can enter a domain name and Spyfu will give you a whole slew of information about that website, including it's organic search ranking for related keywords and information on the websites that compete with that website. It will show how many keywords that website is buying on Adwords, and even what those keywords are.

A good deal of the information is free (there may be a limit on how many searches you can do at a time), but they do make you pay for more specific information. Still, you can get a lot of info for free from them.

Similarweb.com is another free tool that will give you a lot of analysis about a competitor's website that you can use for your own research purposes.

It will show PPC data for the site, but also display ad data from other websites that the company might have advertised on.

They also show audience interest information that is kind of neat; though I have no idea where they get that information or how reliable it is.

Those are just a few good free tools to get you started. Once you dive into them, you'll have more information than you know what to do with; but you'll also start to learn about your potential market and can go from there.

There are also a lot of tools that will research social media stuff for you. Those tools can be useful, but almost always cost money... sometimes quite a bit of money.

I've never been a huge social media guy, so I don't use them all that much.

But, for instance, if you're building a content creation company and plan to build an audience and sell ads...then you need to know what's trending in the social media world about whatever topic you choose to build your business around.

Those tools are great for

brainstorming content ideas because they show you what kinds of content have already gone viral in any specific niche.

You'll want to create similar content with the hope that it too will go viral.

They'll also show you what kind of content sucks and doesn't get passed around very often. So you'll know to stay away from creating similar content. Buzzsumo.com is a good place to start. You'll pay, but they offer a free tier with limited functionality to entice you.

Finally, one of the best things to do is just to go to Google and type in keywords related to your product.

What sorts of websites come up? What do those sites look like? What kinds of products are they selling and how much are they charging?

Do they blog? What sorts of articles do they post on their blog? Do they have a strong social media presence? If so what sorts of things do they post there?

You can learn a lot just by snooping around using Google and some elbow grease.

However you do it, either by hanging out at web forums related to your products, or checking out Facebook groups related to your product, or by using the tools that I just described... you need to systematically and continually research your market and your completion if you want to stay ahead of the curve and win!

CHAPTER THIRTEEN

***

BUSINESS STRUCTURES

Now we need to spend just a few minutes on business structures. I saved this for last because no one wants to deal with this boring shit. Chances are, you've grown bored with this book by now and stopped reading anyway! Who really reads books anyway?

Basically, whenever you form any sort of business (be it online or offline), you need to actually fill out the correct government forms and *actually start a company.*

Many people just sort of jump in without bothering to form an actual company. Those people are called "Sole Proprietors", meaning it's just them...there's no business structure wrapped around them. Another word for them is amateurs!

Sole proprietors often use their own regular personal checking account to handle money, register domain names in their own names, etc etc.

Being a sole proprietor is a terrible idea, for a lot of different reasons.

The two main reasons are liability and taxes.

As a sole proprietor, you're responsible for all the taxes of the business personally, and you're also liable for everything; meaning, if one of your customers chokes on your widget, they can sue you personally...go after your life savings, your house, your car, all your possessions...everything.

On the other hand, if you form an actual company, you can shield yourself from personal liability. The customer sues *your company*, not you. They generally can't come after your car or house or savings, they can only go after the assets in the company.

Businesses in America also get lots of favorable tax deductions that may not be available to you as a sole proprietor.

In many cases, forming a company can be cheap, easy, and quick. You don't need a fancy office (or any office), you don't need letterhead, or employees. It can just be you working out of your kitchen table.

There are basically two types of businesses that you should choose between; a corporation or a limited liability company (LLC).

These are two very different entities and we'll take a moment or two to discuss them both.

Corporations

A corporation is a wholly unique entity, and it is treated as its own person – totally apart from you personally. A corporation is owned by shareholders, who elect a board of directors, who hire managers, who run the company. These designations are important.

You can be all of those things. For instance, when you form the corporation you become the sole shareholder. As the sole shareholder, you elect yourself Chairman of the board of directors. As Chairman of the board, you can then hire yourself as CEO of the company (though you don't have to).

Here's where it gets a little tricky. You are no longer self employed anymore; you are now an employee of the corporation. That means you have to handle payroll taxes just like you would if you were in any other job.

What's more, the corporation has to file its own taxes every year, and match all of your payroll taxes. That means you're going to have to hire the services of a CPA (certified public accountant) to at least file your corporate taxes for you.

This may seem crappy, and it is...but on the flip side, your corporation gets to deduct all sorts of things (like most or all business expenses) and CPA's will file your taxes for you for just a couple hundred bucks...they aren't all that expensive relatively speaking.

Because of those deductions I mentioned, the tax liability of a corporation can often be better than as a sole proprietor.

The problem with corporations is that they generally cost a little more to form, there are more expenses to keep them running each year (like annual report fees, corporate tax filing fees, registered agent fees, and the like), and there's a lot more paperwork involved both at the beginning when you form them and over the years as well.

Limited Liability Companies

A limited liability company (or LLC as they're referred to) is sort of like a hybrid between a corporation and a sole proprietor and probably a little better suited to you as a dot com lifestyle type business owner.

There are no shareholders, instead LLC owners are referred to as "members" (but it basically amounts to the same thing). There is also no board of directors.

Unlike corporations, you will likely not become an "employee" of the LLC (though technically you could if you wanted to – but you won't want to). Instead, all of the income that the LLC generates simply passes through to you.

LLC's are often called "pass through entities".

Instead of filing separate corporate taxes, you simply declare the income on your own personal tax return using a Schedule C and a Schedule SE (both forms you can download from the IRS and both are super easy to fill out).

But just like a corporation, your

LLC gets all kinds of cool tax deductions.

And also like a corporation, an LLC will shield you from personal liability in case someone sues you.

LLC's often cost less to form than a corporation and the annual fees and paperwork to keep them running year after year are almost always less (or non-existent).

Corporation and LLC formation are done at the State Government level, and each state has different laws and rules and fees to start them.

These rules and fees can be DRAMATICALLY different from state to state.

One state might charge $800 to form an LLC and $500 annually to keep it running, while another state might charge $50 to form and $0 annually.

You'll want to research states because you DON'T have to form a corporation or LLC in the state that you live in…you can form them in any state you want!

Generally if you form one outside your own state you just need to hire a registered agent in whatever particular state you want to form your company in. Registered agents merely collect mail on your behalf in whatever state they are in and usually cost anywhere from $50 to $100 a year.

The logic being; you need someone in the state where the company is formed to accept incoming mail in case someone sues you or something.

If you form your company in the state that you live in, then you can be the registered agent yourself and you don't have to hire one (because you can collect mail for your company at your own house or office).

How To Form Them

Is forming your own company something you can do on your own? Maybe. Should you do it on your own? Probably not; at least not the first time.

Back in the old days you had to go see an attorney to form a company. These days, not so much.

Today there are tons of websites that will handle everything for you, from filling out and mailing in the forms correctly, to...well...I guess that's it really. :-P

Sites like:

- LegalZoom.com
- BizFilings.com
- MyCorporation.com
- Incorporate.com

...and others will set you up for just a couple hundred dollars (plus whatever your state charges).

You can always just do a Google search for "Incorporation Services" or something like that.

Those are the big sites, there are also lots of smaller niche sites. If you decide to form an LLC in New Mexico, run a Google search for "How to form an LLC in New Mexico" and you'll probably find some smaller local companies that will fill out the paperwork even cheaper than those big name sites like LegalZoom.com

You can also do your own research and fill out the forms yourself. Many states have guides that will teach you everything you need to know. Often the forms are 1-4 pages long and just ask basic questions like "What's the name of your new company", "what's its address", "what's your name and address", "what's the purpose of the company" (to which you can often reply "to engage in all legal forms of business" or something like that. You get the idea.

Tax ID Number

Besides filling out the articles of incorporation or organization with your state, the only other real thing you need to do is grab yourself a

Tax Id Number (sometimes called an Employer Identification Number or EIN).

Remember how I said that Corporations and LLC's are creatures of the State? Well, you also need to let the Federal Government know they exist. They need some way to keep track of you for tax purposes, and the EIN is how they do that.

An EIN is sort of like a social security number for your company. You'll need one no matter what type of company you form (corporation or LLC).

This number is important for tax reporting purposes, but it's also important for lots of other reasons. You'll use it all the time.

Banks will require it to open business checking accounts,

Insurance companies will probably want it, etc etc.

The EIN is the identification number for your business...much like a social security number identifies you as a person.

Luckily, it's very easy to get an EIN number, and it doesn't costs a thing.

You can do it all online in minutes without ever even talking to a human being.

Back in the day, you actually had to call the IRS and wait on hold half the day to get one of these numbers, but these days it's super easy online.

Form SS-4

To get an EIN you just need to fill out form SS-4 with the IRS, and you can do that online.

Run a Google search for SS-4 and you'll get a link to the IRS website page as well as a link to their instructions page if you don't understand something.

The form is one page long, and a little hard to understand in places if you don't really know what you're doing...so read the instructions if you get confused.

When you search for SS-4 at Google, you'll get links to the form itself as well as the SS-4 info page at the IRS.

You don't want to fill out the actual PDF yourself, instead find the link that says "Apply for an EIN online" or something like that.

The IRS's online application is more like a question and answer walkthrough that then spits out a filled out form and zaps it over to the IRS for you.

You'll get your EIN immediately, print it out and write it down!

PRINT OUT THE NUMBER!

When you complete the application, you'll get a confirmation type page with your new EIN. Print that out!!

A lot of banks will want an actual copy of that stupid thing to open checking accounts etc. It's not good enough to just write down the number and give it to them. It's stupid, I know...but they want to see the form.

The IRS website will give you that form to print out and then it'll say something like "And we'll also mail you a copy of this within 10 days" or some shit.

More often than not, it never shows up in the mail. Bureaucracy.

So print it out at the time you apply. Hold on to it, make copies. Save the PDF to dropbox or evernote.

CHAPTER FOURTEEN

***

SUMMING IT ALL UP

So here we are, at the end of the book! I hope you got a lot out of it, I enjoyed writing it.

We talked about the five different business models that you can focus on.

We talked about my philosophy of starting small and not investing any money so that you can learn and grow and fail fast and start over as often as needed to you get it right.

We talked about some of my basic marketing philosophies, about the marketing funnel, and how mind-shatteringly important email marketing is to any business.

We talked about marketing research tools that you can use to discover if your product has a market and how tough the competition might be.

We talked about traffic and conversion, Growth Hacking, Internet Marketing, and Copywriting and how amazingly important it is to learn.

Finally, we talked about creating an actual company, forming them in a state, setting up a tax ID number, and all that mind-shatteringly boring stuff!

Some of the stuff we talked about was specific. Where I couldn't be as specific as I might have liked due to space constraints, I tried to point you in the right direction to places where you can do a little research. Some of those places cost money (like the cheap copywriting books that I suggested) and others were free (like my offer to give you my Wordpress course over at Codemy.com for free if you use coupon code **dotcom** at checkout).

Hopefully I've sowed the seeds in you to take that leap and dive into the dot com lifestyle.

Like I said, take it slow…don't run out and quit your day job – there's no need to do that! Start small, lean to build a simple Wordpress website, sign up for some affiliate programs and try to growth hack your way to some site traffic. Watch your analytics and see what happens. Learn from everything as you go!

At the end of the day, this stuff is just a lot of fun and I hope that you discover that.

Ultimately I hope you succeed and join me on the beach. There's really nothing else like living the dot com lifestyle. It's not for everyone, but I hope it's for you.

Thanks for reading this book. I hope you got a lot out of it and head over to Codemy.com and shoot me an email if you want to chat about anything you read here. I'm always around and I love helping out whenever I can.

And if you're really into it, sign up for my Codemy.com website. Use that coupon code **elder41** if you sign up for the complete membership and I'll knock $50 bucks off the price.

Good luck!!

Can I Ask You A Quick Favor?

If you enjoyed this book, would you help me out real quick?

Reviews at Amazon literally make or break a book. Just a handful of reviews can vault a book up the best-seller rankings...it's especially important for authors like me who don't have major publishing houses behind them.

If you'd take just a minute or two and head back to Amazon **here**:

www.codemy.com/smart

That will redirect to the book's Amazon page where you can leave a quick review...I'd really appreciate it!

Then head over to Codemy.com and let me know, I'll give you a little something for your efforts ;-)

Thanks again for reading this book, I'd love to hear about your dot com successes! Good luck!

THE END

John Elder

All material contained in this book is for
informational purposes only and is no substitute
for professional advice. Neither John Elder,
Codemy.com or it's affiliates (collectively referred
to as COMPANY) make any guarantees of the
tactics or strategies described in this book.
Successful use of any tactic or strategy described
in this book depends on the specific person, their
experience, and their business and marketing
ability. COMPANY makes no claims or
guarantees regarding income generated from the
use of any tactic or strategy described in this book.
Reader agrees to indemnify and hold COMPANY
harmless from and against any and all claims,
demands, liabilities, expenses, losses, damages,
attorney fees arising from any and all claims and
lawsuits for libel, slander, copyright, and
trademark violation as well as all other claims
resulting from reading this book.

John Elder